DAVID COLEMAN

PARENTING IS CHILD'S PLAY

HOW TO GIVE YOUR CHILD THE BEST START IN LIFE – AND TO HAVE FUN DOING IT

for

Michèle, Conall, Megan and Éanna

PENGUIN IRELAND

Published by the Penguin Group

Penguin Ireland, 25 St Stephen's Green, Dublin 2, Ireland (a division of Penguin Books Ltd)

Penguin Books Ltd, 80 Strand, London WC2R 0RL, England

Penguin Group (USA) Inc., 375 Hudson Street, New York, New York 10014, USA

Penguin Group (Australia), 250 Camberwell Road, Camberwell, Victoria 3124, Australia
(a division of Pearson Australia Group Pty Ltd)

Penguin Group (Canada), 90 Eglinton Avenue East, Suite 700, Toronto, Ontario, Canada M4P 2Y3

(a division of Pearson Penguin Canada Inc.)

Penguin Books India Pvt Ltd, 11 Community Centre, Panchsheel Park, New Delhi - 110 017, India

Penguin Group (NZ), 67 Apollo Drive, Rosedale, North Shore 0632, New Zealand

(a division of Pearson New Zealand Ltd)

Penguin Books (South Africa) (Pty) Ltd, 24 Sturdee Avenue, Rosebank, Johannesburg 2196, South Africa

Penguin Books Ltd, Registered Offices: 80 Strand, London WC2R 0RL, England

www.penguin.com

First published 2007
1

Set in News Gothic and Din Condensed
Printed in China by Leo Paper Group

A CIP catalogue record for this book is available from the British Library

ISBN 978-1-844-88140-6

DAVID COLEMAN is a husband and father of three children. In his spare time he is a clinical psychologist who works with children, teenagers and their families who experience a range of emotional or behavioural difficulties. As well as doing counselling and therapy with children and teenagers, David also supervises, and offers consultation to, others who work with children and families. He gives lectures and facilitates workshops around Ireland on topics such as parenting, bullying, communicating with children and dealing with challenging behaviour.

David is the presenter of the popular RTÉ television programme *Families in Trouble*, in which he gets stuck in to help parents sort out different issues they have with their children's behaviour. He also contributes regularly to radio and print media on children, childhood issues and parenting. This is his first book.

CONTENTS

INTRODUCTION

Having children is a big challenge and a huge responsibility, but nobody says it can't be fun too. It might sound unlikely to describe it as child's play, but parenting can be a truly positive experience when your child respects you and responds to what you ask. And your child is more likely to respect you and respond to you when you have built a positive relationship based on fun and consistency. When our children are happy and having fun we tend to be happier and have more fun too. Contented children don't have too many behaviour problems!

The good news is that there are things we can do to make the whole process of rearing children easier. And in this book I am going to tell you what they are

Parenting can be child's play but – and of course there's a 'but' – it's just not always easy. Since our children don't come with instruction manuals most of us approach parenting on the basis of trial and error. Although this is a good enough approach to parenting, the trouble starts when we don't realize that we are making errors, or when we do realize it, but just can't figure how to make things right. The good news is that there are things we can do to make the whole process of rearing children easier. And in this book I am going to tell you what they are and how you can apply them to your own situation.

Parenting is Child's Play focuses on the first six years of the game of growing with your children. It explains the basic gist of what that game is about and it will help you to develop specific rules to guide your own fun in playing.

I'm not interested in perfection in parenting – for the simple reason that we are human and by our nature humans are imperfect. That means we'll make mistakes in lots of areas, including how we raise our children. I only have the nerve to write a book like this because I know I have messed it up myself on many an occasion and I'm still learning as I go. In the book you get not just my experience and knowledge as a child psychologist but you also get my wisdom (limited as it may be) from my trial and error with my own three children. Hopefully, the book will provide you with the information to be able to spot when you do make mistakes and some ideas for what else to do instead.

I'm not going to be worried if your child doesn't eat all their greens (they don't need to); or if your daughter wakes four times in the night (all children come to wakefulness; most just learn to soothe themselves back to sleep); or your boy cries for your attention (without words how else will he do it?); or your toddler eats with their fingers (the feel of food is important for developing brains); or your five-year-old melts down on day one of school (starting so much newness is unsettling). What I'll be suggesting to you throughout the book is that you don't have to get worried about these things either. The biggest factor that often maintains children's 'problem behaviours' is parental anxiety and over-involvement. I'll guide you in how and when to sit back, relax and only get involved when absolutely necessary.

How you treat your child in the first six years of life will set a strong and sometimes indelible pattern for your interactions with them through the rest of their childhood. Your relationship with your child is central to everything else you do. It will dictate how you approach every problem or challenge that they or life presents to you. Even though that relationship is so important we never really pay it much attention. We expect to be able to rely on instinct to 'know' what to say or do in our interactions with our children. The only trouble with that is that our instinctual responses are often determined by how we ourselves were parented; for good or for bad. I'll show you how to add to your instinct with some guaranteed ways of improving your relationship with your child and increasing the quality of your communication with them.

I know being a parent is not simply an oochy-coochy, huggy, smiles-in-the-garden love-in with your children

In case you think I'm getting all airy fairy and losing touch with the real world let me quickly assure you that I know being a parent is not simply an oochy-coochy, huggy, smiles-in-the-garden love-in with your children. There are lots of times when you have to be firm, but fair, and let your child know that the world does not revolve around them.

Children, and especially the under-sixes, love routine, consistency and predictability

Indeed, one of the biggest mistakes we make as parents is to believe that we have to appease our children's wants all of the time. Our children need limits to be imposed on their behaviour, sometimes just for their safety and sometimes to ensure fairness and equity for everyone. Without limits children learn omnipotence, i.e., they believe that they are central, and everyone exists solely to do their bidding. Of course, the world isn't like that, and we have a responsibility as parents to gently but definitely teach our children that some things are OK and some things are not OK.

Most of what I'm suggesting to you in this book is not new or ground-breaking. All the basics of good parenting are out there already. The central core of what we need to achieve is to be consistent. No matter what you are doing, whether it be catching your child being good or responding to them when they are bold, you've got to respond in a predictable way every time. Children, and especially the under-sixes, love routine, consistency and predictability. Children who know what to expect from their parents will be less anxious and more able to develop trusting and secure attachments. Your job as a parent will be way easier when your child has security in their relationship with you.

In the book, along with a load of good stuff on building relationships and bonds with your baby and young child, I've covered all the typical tough spots of early parenting: temper tantrums, general behaviour management (for things like hitting or biting), sleeping problems, toilet-training, eating problems and coping with childcare and school. The advice is practical and based on experience of what works. The advice is also child-centred, i.e., it assumes that your child will be the best guide to what they need and that you will respond to that. Throughout the book, which I have broken up into nine chapters, I'll be using examples of the situations we parents get into and how we get out of them again, both successfully and unsuccessfully.

No matter how good we are, our children will always do something that will leave us pulling our hair out and wondering what we are going to do. Hopefully you'll find the answers inside. If you don't find the answers to your particular issue here then just ask your mammy – and do the opposite (only joking!).

So if you love your child and you want to do the very best job you can in parenting them, then make a nice cup of tea and read on ...

So if you love your child and you want to do the very best job you can in parenting them, then make a nice cup of tea and read on ...

IMPROVING COMMUNICATION

IT AIN'T WHAT YOU SAY, IT'S THE WAY THAT YOU SAY IT

With children it is crucial to remember that we communicate by what we say, how we say it, what we do while we are saying it and what we do when we aren't even intending to communicate. The messages we give to our children from the moment of their birth are powerful. They have the power to nurture, console, enliven, encourage, excite and motivate. They also have the power to hurt, reject, confuse, terrify and anger. How we communicate with our children will strengthen our bond and attachment with them or it can destroy or block that attachment. It pays, therefore, to be alert to what we communicate and also to understand better what our children communicate to us.

I think it is no harm to use skills and techniques to bolster that attachment through communication. Why shouldn't we, as parents, use what is well established to improve the way we listen to our children? We can also ensure that we give them the messages we intend rather than messages that get transmitted unknowingly.

Loads of parents who come to talk to me about their teenagers bemoan the lack of communication that they have with them. I often try to track back with those parents to the times when their child was much younger (as a baby and toddler) to explore the quality of their communication and relationship. What I find is that, even when the children were small, those parents struggled to get messages across to their child, and their child frequently relied on their behaviour to communicate with their parent.

They may show you that they are angry by having a tantrum; they may show you that they are upset by having a sulk; they may show you that they are frustrated by becoming aggressive

If children don't have understanding of their feelings, or don't have the words and language to express their feelings, then it is highly likely that they will express those feelings through their behaviour.

Some examples of this might be that they may show you that they are angry by having a tantrum; they may show you that they are upset by having a sulk; they may show you that they are frustrated by becoming aggressive. When they are under six, this can often be understandable. A two-year-old certainly won't have the command of language to express feelings articulately. By the time they are twelve, though, we do expect children to be more articulate. Unless we begin early, however, our children don't learn the language or the expectation that we have that they should deal with their feelings by talking them through rather than by behaving 'badly'.

So I have set out a range of skills and ideas about communication in this chapter. I want you to be able to think about what messages you give your child through not just the words you use but also the non-verbal behaviour you employ. Once you have an idea of the skills you can use I am going to show you how you can use them to actively listen to your child and thereby dramatically improve the quality, tone and effectiveness of your communication with them.

THIS CHAPTER LOOKS AT ...

What gets communicated – the role of non-verbal behaviour in communication

How it gets communicated – the role of paraverbal behaviour (all the aspects of speech except the words used)

Active listening – encouraging communication with your child by showing you are paying them attention and hearing what they are trying to communicate to you

WHAT GETS COMMUNICATED

How many times have we had big rows with our children where we end up screaming at them at top volume as we drag them along the corridor or up the stairs to their bedroom? Lots? After all, 'giving out' would be the speciality subject of most parents if they ended up on *Mastermind*. Most of us have it down to a fine art. Often our 'giving out' coincides with the height of our toddler's temper tantrum, and between the two of us we are probably raising the roof with the volume and frustration that is expressed.

Research shows that when we are in a crisis situation like that, i.e., a big row, only 7 per cent of the meaning that our children will take from what we are saying comes from the words that we actually use. This seems like a shockingly small percentage. It also begs the question, if they are not taking meaning from what we are saying, what are they taking meaning from? The answer is they take the rest of their meaning from the non-verbal behaviour that we use while we are talking and also from things like the tone of our voice while we are talking. Children, when they are being given out to, take 55 per cent of the meaning of what's being said to them from the non-verbal behaviour of their parent or caregiver. Another 38 per cent of what they understand from what we are saying comes from things like tone of voice. So it's really important that we understand how these two elements impact on our communication.

If they are not taking meaning from what we are saying, what are they taking meaning from?

We engage in lots of different non-verbal behaviours while we are talking and communicating. They include things like our eye contact, the gestures that we make, the facial expressions that we have, our positioning relative to the person we are talking to and our posture relative to the person we are talking to. These things affect all of our communication whether we are talking with other adults or with children. So you can use the tips and skills that I am about to give you with your husband, wife or partner as well as with your tiny tots. Let's look at each of those non-verbal behaviours in a bit more detail.

EYE CONTACT

Our eyes are a really important and crucial element of our communication. Being able to look into somebody else's eyes while they are talking or while you're talking gives us so much extra information about whether they are listening or not and what they are feeling about what we are saying that we place great emphasis upon it in social communication.

You probably noticed that when your baby was very small they spent most of their time looking into your eyes. Studies into tiny babies and their gazing behaviour show that once they can begin to focus (at about six weeks of age) they are drawn to their caregivers' eyes. Using technology, researchers have tracked small babies' eye movements and found that, while their gaze will track across the whole face, most of their time is spent looking into the eyes of their caregiver. So even from early on humans are instinctively drawn to making eye contact as a way of increasing connection and intimacy in communication.

It's almost as if we have an instinctual belief that the eyes are the gateway to the soul. So when we really want to connect to someone we look them in the eye. We also use our beliefs about the power of eye contact to determine if someone is lying: 'Look

Even from early on humans are instinctively drawn to making eye contact as a way of increasing connection and intimacy in communication

me in the eye when you say that!' Our assumption is that the other person will not be able to hold our gaze as they look back at us if they are lying. Small children playing hide and seek will believe that they are hidden from your view so long as their eyes are covered. Their thinking must be: 'If you can't see my eyes then you can't see "me".'

There are two simple social rules to eye contact in communication in our western culture. If you can remember them, it will make your talking and listening much more effective. The first rule is: when you are listening to someone always try to make eye contact. Even if the person who is talking to you isn't looking at you it is important that you are looking at them and ready to make eye contact whenever they glance back at you. Think again how many times you have said to your four-year-old, 'Look at me while I am talking to you.' Why do we say that? We say it because, when somebody looks at us, it is a really strong indication that they are actually listening to us. If they continue to look away, we (probably rightly) assume that they aren't paying attention to us and are focused instead on whatever it is they are looking at.

The second rule is: when you are talking, you don't have to make eye contact with the other person all of the time and in fact if you do make eye contact all of the time it can be a little bit off-putting. Usually, when a talker makes eye contact all of the time with the listener it's an attempt to either express intimacy or as a challenge to conflict.

When your three-year-old is tugging at your leg trying to get your attention, what they really want from you often is just for you to look at them

The classic situations would be either two lovers sitting across a table looking deep into each other's eyes as they murmur loving words to each other or two people who are having a row, 'eyeballing' each other. In the case of the lovers it is as if the openness in eye contact is designed to say, 'I am hiding nothing from you. You have an open window to my heart and I have to yours.' In the second situation of the row there is an unspoken message like 'I'm not going to give in first.' Whoever does flinch in the staring contest is also more likely to defer to the other person and lose the fight.

It's really important for us as parents to remember these rules. When your three-year-old is tugging at your leg trying to get your attention, what they really want from you often is just for you to look at them. Once you look at them, then they know that you are paying attention to them. If you keep working at the counter-top, for example, while they are trying to talk to you, it is quite likely they are going to realize that your attention is split between what you are doing and what they are saying and they are likely to get quite frustrated and angry about that. But by making eye contact with them you can often offset that frustration and give them a clear message that you are now attending to them and that you are now ready to listen to them.

The other side of this, as I mentioned earlier, is that, if you want to know that your child is listening to you, the most efficient way to know that is to see if they are looking at you while you are talking to them. That's why, if you want to be sure that you have their attention, it's often a good idea to go to them and, if needs be, turn their head towards you as you speak. If their eyes are on the telly, there is a good chance that's where their attention is also. But if their eyes are on you, then you are much more likely to have them listening to you also.

GESTURES

I think we often underestimate the importance of the gestures that we make to our children. Sometimes the gestures we make are unconscious. Examples might be a shrug of the shoulders, a dismissive wave of the hand or a wagging, scolding finger. On the positive side, we will also often throw our arms wide open to invite our toddlers to come in for a big hug. Or, as you sit down, you might pat your knee, again inviting your child to come and sit there for a nice cuddle.

I often give talks to parents and people working with children and use the following exercise with them when I am talking about communication. I get everybody to make the 'OK' sign by putting their right hand up in the air and joining the thumb and forefinger to make an O. Then I get everybody in the room to wave their arm vigorously from side to side. I then tell them in a clear voice to place that 'OK' sign on to their nose but at the same time I am demonstrating a different action by bringing my hand down on to my cheek.

About 80 per cent of the audience generally copy what I have done and have their hand on their cheek, even though I have just told them to put their hand on to their nose. Very quickly people realize that their hand is in the wrong place and they begin to slide it across their face on to their nose, looking a bit sheepish and looking at the people around them to see where their hands are. There is usually a great deal of embarrassed laughter amongst the audience as they realize that very few of them have actually followed my verbal instruction.

Even though it is a bit of a cheap psychological trick, it does demonstrate the very powerful role of gestures. The point of the exercise is to show people that we are much more likely to do what someone else does rather than what someone says. Eighty per cent of the audience copy my actions rather than follow my instructions. It's not reasonable, therefore, to expect your child to do what you say if you then go on to do something that's different from that yourself.

What we do is so much more powerful and noticeable than what we say and so we can use this to role-model for our children what we expect of them. In our house, for example, we expect our children to carry their dishes over to the counter after their meal (because 'everyone helps the family' is a value we promote!). I am possibly the most likely to leave mine on the table and get distracted with something else. My wife kindly reminds me every time, not because she isn't prepared to carry my empty plate but because she knows how important it is that our children see me doing (role-modelling) what she and I tell them all the time.

What we do is so much more powerful and noticeable than what we say

Don't be fooled into thinking that children don't notice, either. Our children are alert to our every move and are constantly trying to make sense of it and understand it. They will have analysed, for example, our reactions to common situations and will know how we generally respond. My own mother tells a story about how she was driving along with me and my brother in the back of the car. My brother was about four at the time. Another car overtook her and pulled in right in front, causing my mum to brake suddenly. My brother, allegedly, piped up from the back something to the effect of 'Isn't this when you are supposed to shake your fist at him and call him a f**king b*****d?' I'm never sure whose driving etiquette he was supposedly emulating, but he learned it somewhere and he learned it from observation.

FACIAL EXPRESSION

Once you start talking and thinking about non-verbal behaviour suddenly you become aware of so many things that always happen that are just part of our natural communication. For example, I am sure you have had the experience of telling somebody something and then noticing the surprise, shock, disbelief, delight, amazement, pride, upset or other feeling being displayed openly on their face. The true reaction of a person is often visible in their face milliseconds before their verbal reaction comes out.

Can you remember it with your own parents? The first time you told them that you had a boyfriend or girlfriend, for example, that slight opening of their eyes registering their surprise and maybe shock was quickly covered up by their response to you, which was probably something along the lines of how delighted they were for you. Then fast-forward the years to think about your own little toddler: you are asking them how the crayon marks got on the wall, and the words that come out are 'I don't know', but their face displays all the guilt and the fear of your reaction when you eventually find out that it was them.

It's really helpful for us to be able to be in charge of our facial expressions and not to let them give away our true feeling all of the time. You may feel hugely frustrated, angry or upset with something your child has done, but it's not always helpful to let your children know that straight away.

> It's really helpful for us to be able to be in charge of our facial expressions and not to let them give away our true feeling all of the time

You may find it helpful to just become more aware as you talk with other people about what your face is doing. For example, are you an eyebrow-raiser? Do you take on a particular frown or grimace as you concentrate? When you smile, does your mouth come open? Are your teeth visible? The more aware you are of what your face does the more able you'll be to control it to suit your needs.

It's a great feeling when you get to the stage that, when your child asks you whether they can have a treat, for example, all you have to do is give a single-raised-eyebrow response which communicates very effectively the whole message 'Are you being serious? There is not a hope in hell of you getting a treat after the way you have been behaving all day!', and then your child in response to your raised eyebrow casts their eyes downward and shuffles off feeling sheepish. That's assuming, of course, that the same raised eyebrow doesn't thrust them into an apoplectic fit of rage and frustration at your refusal to give them what they want.

POSITIONING AND POSTURE

I am willing to bet that at some stage in your childhood you stood in a principal's office, maybe with your knees knocking a bit, while the principal sat impassively behind the desk in their big chair. That moment was probably bad enough, with the large imposing desk giving an air of authority to the figure behind it. But then, when the principal gets up out of their chair and stands a good foot if not two above you, that power and authority can become even more threatening. We need to remember things like this when we are dealing with our own children.

Children aged six and under are usually about three and a half foot and under in height. Most of us adults range between five to six and a half feet in height. This means that, when we stand up in relation to our child, we also can cut a very imposing figure. We can use this to our advantage sometimes to really bring home the message about who's boss in the situation. But also, if you have a child who is sitting in a crumpled little heap, boo-hooing their eyes out, it's much more effective to go and squat down beside them, so that you are closer to their eye level, to make eye contact. Your posture then will show comforting and caring.

Do you remember the example I gave earlier of your three-year-old tugging at your leg while you are working at the counter-top in the kitchen? Simply by turning towards them to listen you are using your posture and your positioning to show your child that you are paying them attention. All before you say a word.

I have met lots of parents in the course of my work who have told me about how their child 'needs to be told ten times to do something' before they respond or react. In most cases, when I question them a little bit about those situations, I discover that the first nine times that they asked they were shouting from the kitchen when their child was in the living room. It was only on the tenth occasion that they actually came into the living room (often in a fury) to stand in front of their child and ensured that they had their child's attention before the message was given and received.

We do get infuriated if our children seem to ignore us. It is quite possible, however, that, if our children are in watching television or are playing away and engrossed in a game, they won't be able to split their attention to notice us and our call. When they are small, it is rare that they are deliberately ignoring us. It is much more likely that they are just busy and distracted by something else more engaging than us and our request. But over years a pattern can emerge where they do ignore us for the first nine times because they know that it is only on the tenth time that we'll ensure that they listen.

I think because we are parents and we are adults we often feel that our children should come to us, but actually it often makes more sense for us to go to them

I think because we are parents and we are adults we often feel that our children should come to us, but actually it often makes more sense for us to go to them. At worst it will reduce our own frustration and at best it shows that we respect our children enough to make the effort of coming to them when we have something important to say. In fact, even as I write this, I am reminded of the number of people who have also said to me that they have got into terrible power and control battles with their child: 'Come in here now while I am speaking to you!' Often, whatever the original issue was is overcome by the battle that ensues as you try to exert your power to force your child to come to you. Again, this kind of power battle is needless and can be avoided by thinking about your positioning, not theirs.

HOW YOU COMMUNICATE

The next most important thing to consider is how your voice sounds and how the information is being communicated. If you remember, during times of crises, like in a row, 38 per cent of the meaning that your child takes from what you say comes from how your voice sounds. This includes things like the tone of your voice, the cadence or rhythm of your speech and the loudness of your voice. Once you begin to think about it, and pay some attention to it, you begin to realize just how much extra information we give with the sound of our voices. Usually, the context of an event will dictate things like the tone of voice, loudness and so on.

For example, if you happen to be back in your kitchen, and your toddler comes running in, trips over his own feet, sprawls to the floor and starts screaming, you are very likely to go over, be comforting and say something like 'Are you all right?' in gentle, warm tones. Obviously the intention here is to comfort and soothe, and we will indicate that in how we sound. In a different context, take the example of when our toddler comes running into the kitchen already screaming in frustration and then physically throws himself to the floor in front of us. We may well feel indignant, amazed or bemused and indeed bewildered by his choice of behaviour. The tone of the same question, 'Are you all right?', will reflect this. So, that same question, spoken with that bewildered tone, could actually be interpreted to mean 'Are you for real?' or 'What's come over you all of a sudden?' or 'Are you OK in the head, throwing yourself to the floor?'

Another good example of how we change tone is in how we respond to babies. Think of the sing-song lyrical tone that you use with tiny babies. You might be telling them that

you have to disturb them to change their nappy but you are saying it with a lightness and ease because you are instinctively aware that your baby will be more aware of how you sound rather than what you are saying.

We can also use the cadence or rhythm of our speech to make different meanings. Try asking the question 'What is going on here?' in the following two ways. In the first instance say it as if you are genuinely interested to find out what's going on here because it looks like it's fun and you might like to be involved. The chances are you will ask the question quickly, probably shortening words down to 'What's goin' on here?' and raising the pitch of your voice on the last word. Now practise asking the same question imagining a situation where you know full well what's happened and you're extremely unhappy about what's happened, as when you walk into the bathroom to find that your toddler has been doing 'water play' and has managed to block the sink and flood the floor. My guess is that the sentence will come out much slower, with pauses between each word, and with a good stern tone thrown in for good measure: 'What – is – going – on – here?'

This rhythm of our speech fluctuates all the time from quick-moving, sing-song-like rhythms for the easy-going, fun times to the slow, deliberate enunciation when there is going to be trouble. It doesn't take our children long to learn that you're in a different mood depending on how you're speaking.

Often we speak more loudly when we want to catch someone's attention, or if we feel that we are not being heard because of other sounds around. Paradoxically, sometimes when you are in a group it is more effective to talk quietly in order to get the silence required from other people. If people are expecting you to speak, and you then begin to speak quietly, they tend to become quieter themselves in order to be able to listen and to hear what you are trying to say. In contrast, if you begin to talk more and more loudly in the group, sometimes people will also raise the volume of their own conversation in order to be able to continue above you.

> It doesn't take our children long to learn that you're in a different mood depending on how you're speaking

The difficulty we face as parents is in controlling our volume in the midst of our own feelings. Because, when we get angry and frustrated (which can be a regular enough occurrence when you have got small children), we also tend to become more loud in talking to, or indeed shouting at, them. Getting loud, however, can be counter-productive. For a start it gives your child a message that, when you are angry and frustrated, you just shout as loudly as you can (after all, that's what Mam and Dad are doing). Also, the louder you get, the more your child is likely to be tuning in only to things like your non-verbal behaviour and the tone of your voice rather than the actual words that you are trying to pass on.

So, if you have an important message to convey to your child, you are best off doing it in a calm, slow and considerate way. I say this, of course, in the full knowledge that I have been guilty of many shouts and roars at my own children. I get frustrated and then it is only in hindsight that I remember that the point I was trying to make has been completely lost in the midst of my own anger and frustration. That's the joy of being human. We all make mistakes. The challenge to us, however, is to come back every time and be more thoughtful in how and what we are communicating to our children.

So, if you have an important message to convey to your child, you are best off doing it in a calm, slow and considerate way

ACTIVE LISTENING

So let's assume that we can manage to spend a good portion of our time outside of those crisis situations where we are arguing with our children. That means that when we talk regularly we can hope that more than 7 per cent of the meaning they're taking is coming from the words that we are using. So let's focus on what we can do with the words now.

We want to show our children that we are listening to what they say and that what they say is important, valuable and being attended to. Active listening is the method by which we can do this.

Sometimes we may think that listening is a passive task, after all you are just sitting there while somebody else is speaking. The reality is, however, that listening is not passive at all. There are things we do to encourage someone to keep talking and to show them that we are really listening to them. We give focused attention, we verbally encourage, we reflect back or echo what we hear, we summarize what we have heard, we clarify what we have heard, we ask open questions, we incorporate feelings into the conversation and we stay silent sometimes. Let's look at how each of these skills works in practice.

FOCUSED ATTENTION

The first step to showing that you are listening to someone is to focus your attention on them. If you think back to some of the things we talked about in using our non-verbal behaviour you will recall that the easiest way to give focused attention is to turn to face the person who's talking and look them in the eye. It may mean that you stop whatever other task you were doing. It may mean that you ask other people around to be quiet. It may also mean that you have to be quiet yourself.

The experience of being attended to in this way is very powerful for any child. And this is the kind of attention that most children will want most of the time. The reality is that we can't give it all of the time, so in the times when we are going to give it to them we may as well be 100 per cent with them when we are doing it.

Even when children themselves seem almost too young to communicate, as tiny infants, we still end up attending to them in this way. Think back to all those times when your toddlers and small children were babies. Can you remember when you were changing their nappy, and they gurgled, and you stopped everything, you turned or moved to make sure that your face was directly over theirs and you gurgled back to them? Or how about the times when they were three months old, and you lay them on their back to kick while you busied yourself with other tasks? Then, when they let out their first cry, you came over to them, maybe picked them up but at the very least looked down at them and checked in warm and caring tones how they were doing. If, in the same situation, you had kept going with the task and had simply called to your tiny baby it wouldn't have let them know that you were paying attention to them.

Small children love to be attended to. And if we are really interested in listening to them, then we have to stop what else we are doing and focus on them while we are listening.

ENCOURAGING

When we are listening to someone, we instinctively make encouraging noises and gestures to indicate to the other person that we'd like them to keep talking. Examples of this are how you'll be nodding your head, smiling, saying 'uh uh' and 'I know'. These may seem like tiny things, but without them the experience of a talker is lessened.

In our society and culture we have become so used to this that sometimes if we don't get this kind of feedback we think that somebody has stopped listening. The easiest example of this might be when you are on the telephone and suddenly realize that as you are talking there is a complete silence on the other end of the line. This is the point at which many of us will stop talking to check if the other person is still there. And in response, the other person quickly goes, 'Yeah, yeah, I was just listening …' Because you can't see the person you don't get any non-verbal feedback like eye contact or head nodding to know if they are paying you attention and you are reliant on those little sounds of encouragement.

In some of the workshops that I run for parents and professionals working with children I get them to practise all the skills of communication. In one of the exercises that we do I get them to sit in pairs with their backs to each other. One person of each pair is designated as the 'talker', and I ask them to talk about, for example, the last holiday that they were on. The other person is designated as the 'listener' and they are instructed to not make any sound or any movement while the 'talker' is talking (remember they have their back to the 'talker' too). I give all the pairs five minutes to 'chat'.

In the exercise, when the 'listeners' give no encouragement (either verbal or non-verbal) most 'talkers' dry up after about a minute. At the end of the exercise I get the group to discuss the experience. During this discussion the 'talkers' usually describe how difficult it was to keep talking when they felt the other person wasn't listening. They explain that they didn't feel listened to because they were getting no feedback and no encouragement from them.

For our children, therefore, we clearly want to enrich their experience of talking to us, and the easiest way to do this is by giving lots of non-verbal and verbal encouragement and feedback.

REFLECTING/ECHOING

When our children talk to us, we find ourselves frequently repeating what they are saying. Sometimes it is an exact replication of what they say and other times it is a variation on it. In terms of communication skills this is known as echoing (repeating exactly) and reflecting (saying back a slight variation of what was said to you). Doing this may seem a pointless task and not much of a way to communicate. In fact, it is a great help to someone talking as it allows them to know that you have heard them. After all, if you can repeat it, you must have heard it.

Ignore any of those people who tell you not to gurgle and goo at babies

With tiny babies we reflect and echo almost constantly. It is part of the turn-taking that we engage in with babies. They 'goo, goo'; we also 'goo, goo'. Ignore any of those people who tell you not to gurgle and goo at babies. If babies make a sound, try to copy it. Every sound they make is part of their development of language. By copying the sounds we let them know that they are being attended to, and it allows them the opportunity to hear back their vocalizations. In general, babies are exposed to lots of language from parents, carers, siblings and other people. Engaging in turn-taking 'babbling' with your baby is good for them. It doesn't confuse them, and they will still learn language. In fact, they are learning the skill of conversation, which involves one person waiting while the other person makes sounds and then taking their turn to make sounds while the other person listens. It just happens that we call some sounds words! Their early sounds just need to be reflected back to them. They don't need them to be corrected.

Mind you, as they grow older they will make sounds that approximate real words, and, if we can guess what those 'words' might be, then it is really helpful to repeat the actual word for your child. So, imagine your twenty-month-old is tugging at your leg, pointing at the fruit bowl and saying 'owah'. In response you might say, 'Orange, you'd like an orange?' (Wouldn't that be a fantasy for lots of us – a child asking for fruit!)

This kind of reflecting is an opportunity to teach your child the words and help them to develop language. I am a big believer in reflecting, echoing and putting words on to the actions, gestures and vocalizations of small children. When we do it, it gives them a great 'leg up' on their language development.

Using reflecting and echoing is also great when your toddler is doing something. Often their actions are trying to give us a message, and it is really helpful for us to translate that message, or at the very least to encourage our communication with them by simply commenting on what we are seeing. I call this observational commentary. I go through it in some detail in the chapter on play. For now suffice it to say that it involves nothing more than telling your child what you see them doing. So as they lift their cup to their lips you say, 'You are lifting up your cup and drinking.' Equally, if your child is thrashing about on the floor in a tantrum, you could say, 'I see you lying on the floor, kicking it with your feet.' It might seem a little trite, but reflecting back to our children what we see gives them important information about what they are doing (that they might not realize) and also shows that we are paying close enough attention to them to be able to tell them what they are doing. Both of these are powerful experiences for children.

SUMMARIZING/CLARIFYING

This is another skill we commonly use in talking that we probably aren't aware of. When someone chats away to us we often will stop them and check bits of the story out. Examples might be 'Really? He said that?' or 'So first you stood out of your chair and then the teacher gave out to you?' or 'Tell me again the order of events.'

With small children we often don't get enough of a story told to us to require summarizing it. But what is more likely to happen is that by us asking a series of questions we get parts of the story, either in correct order or a bit mixed up. Then it is both helpful and educational for us to put them all together to make a complete story in summation. Again, this is also a really powerful message to a child that you have been listening to them. After all, if you had ignored them, you couldn't piece it all together or summarize it. Asking questions to clarify what has been said (because we are either interested or incredulous) is also an expression of our involvement in what our children are telling us.

QUESTIONS

I have a bit of a thing about questions. Even though I have just been advocating asking children questions to clarify what they are telling you, I often feel that, with small children especially, but children generally, questioning them is a bit stressful. There is a social expectation that, if you ask someone a question, then they must answer it. This puts pressure on the person of whom you ask a question. Not only that, but we frequently ask children questions that we already know the answer to, and where only one answer is acceptable. Even when we don't know the answer, it can be stressful for children, who themselves may not be able to answer because they can't express what they need

One of the things we know about small children is that, when they get anxious, they are likely to act it out in bad behaviour rather than express it through words

or want to say. After all, here is an adult expecting an answer that the child can't deliver, and that leads to anxiety. One of the things we know about small children is that, when they get anxious, they are likely to act it out in bad behaviour rather than express it through words. Our questions, therefore, can actually provoke bad behaviour.

If we have to ask questions, I believe we should always try to ask open questions. Open questions are questions that have unlimited potential for answering. The opposite of this, a closed question, is a question that requires a simple 'yes/no' answer. It is amazing how often we ask closed questions. For example: 'Did you knock over the milk?', 'Are you Irish?', 'Do you like sugar in your tea?' The same examples rephrased as open questions would be: 'Who knocked over the milk?', 'Where are you from?', 'What do you like in your tea?'

A short way to remember the difference is that open questions begin with the five 'w's (and a 'h') – who, what, where, why, when and how. They are important because, as the name suggests, they open up conversations. Closed questions can close conversations down. When we converse, one of the skills of encouraging someone to talk more is to ask questions that seek them to expand on a topic or to clarify a topic. Open questions do this more effectively than closed ones.

There are lots of situations where we must ask questions as otherwise we would have no way of finding out information from our children. But with small children we generally know what has been going on for them because they are rarely away from us for very long, or we get a full report of what went on if they have been away in childcare or wherever. So instead, we use questions often as a way of checking whether our children are telling the truth or as a way of giving out to them.

Imagine the scene: a five-year-old, called Seán, has had a bad day in school, and the teacher has mentioned to his mum that she had to give out to him for pushing another child in the class. Our natural reaction to this situation is to subject our child to 'twenty questions' geared towards eliciting the truth, establishing the facts and determining the consequences. I guess a typical conversation might go like this (I've put the unspoken subtext in italics):

Mother: **Did you have a good day in school today?** *(I'd like him to tell me in his own words how bold he was.)*

Seán: **Yeah.** *(Let's see how much she knows.)*

Mother: **Did anything bad happen?** *(Come on, you know there is stuff to own up to.)*

Seán: **No.** *(I'll try gambling that she doesn't know the truth because I didn't see her talking to teacher.)*

Mother: **Are you sure?** *(I'll give him one final chance to be truthful, even though he doesn't deserve it.)*

Seán: **Yeah.** *(I can't admit to lying, that'll just make her mad.)*

Mother: Nothing at all? *(Now I'm just cross because we both know he is lying to me.)*

Seán: No. *(Uh-oh, there's trouble ahead.)*

Mother: Didn't you push one of the other children in class? *(At last we'll get the truth out there.)*

Seán: *(Just gives a shrug and looks away, knowing that all is lost.)*

Mother: Look at me while I'm talking to you. I know you were being bold today, your teacher told me. Did you do it? *(You know I can't bear to be lied to, and yet here you are blatantly lying to my face.)*

Seán: Yeah, maybe. *(I guess I have no choice but to admit it now, maybe it'll take the sting out of her anger.)*

Mother: So why are you lying to me? *(I know why I just want to hear you say it.)*

Seán: Dunno. *(Well, if you can't work it out I'm not telling you.)*

Mother: And anyway what were you messing with the other kids for? *(I never get anywhere with his lying, I'd better go back to his boldness in school.)*

Seán: Dunno. *(Just get the punishment over with. You are obviously not interested in hearing the real story and you probably wouldn't believe me anyway if the teacher has told you.)*

Mother: I don't like you being bold in school and I don't like you lying to me. When your father gets home you are in big trouble. *(I can't stand the way he just clams up. I can't understand why he doesn't tell me what's going on for him. Then I'd be able to help. Instead, we just end up fighting.)*

At this point I guess Seán feels totally frustrated (like his mother) and maybe anxious at the prospect of the impending consequences later. But because he can't express these feelings in words he will probably end up showing them in a tantrum or maybe a poke at his younger sister or stomping off, grumbling, whingeing or complaining. I'd say his frustration stems from feeling trapped in the lie, and feeling unheard in his perception of whatever happened in the classroom earlier. But the particular line of questioning adopted by his mother actually sets him up for the frustration and anxiety he now feels.

A different approach to the same issue could have focused on Seán's behaviour but not by questioning. Imagine a conversation like this:

Mother: I heard from your teacher that there was trouble in your class today. She told me you were pushing another child.

Seán: No, Liam kicked me.

Mother: So you understand that something different happened in the classroom than what the teacher understands.

Seán: Yeah. Liam kept kicking me under the table and I pushed him away.

Mother: So Liam kicked you, and then you pushed Liam, and the teacher saw you.

Seán: Yeah, I guess so.

Mother: It sounds like the teacher didn't realize Liam had been kicking you and that you felt provoked.

Seán: No.

Mother: That's a pity; it sounds a bit unfair to you.

Seán: She never believes me anyway.

Mother: I guess it doesn't seem worthwhile to you to tell her what really happened because you don't think she would believe you.

Seán: Yeah.

Mother: But you need a different way of dealing with kicks from Liam rather than pushing him, because your pushing might have hurt him, and it disturbed the class.

Seán: Maybe, but I didn't hurt him.

Mother: I'm sure you didn't. What else could you have done about Liam kicking you?

Seán: I dunno.

Mother: Well, I think you need to tell the teacher. She is more likely to believe you if you don't go pushing instead.

Seán: Maybe.

Mother: Tomorrow we'll talk to her together to explain what happened today and to share the plan we made for what you'll do in the future if Liam kicks you or provokes you.

Seán: OK so.

Mother: OK so.

The mum in this version was explicit about what was alleged to have happened in the class so that both she and Seán knew where they were starting from. She also didn't deny Seán's experience of the incident but rather acknowledged that he and the teacher could have different perceptions of the same thing. This turned out to be especially important as her son's experience of not being believed by the teacher could easily have been replicated by her. All the way through she tried to see things from his perspective. By not asking questions but simply repeating and summarizing what Seán said, she was able to get a complete picture of what happened from his viewpoint and agreed a plan to resolve similar situations in the future. You'll notice that she didn't punish him; the only consequence is that he will have to sort things out with the teacher with her help.

   The mum in this example used lots of different communication skills, especially active listening, to understand and resolve the situation. Both she and her child leave the conversation feeling satisfied and listened to, and neither of them is frustrated or angry.

KEY POINTS TO REMEMBER

→ In speech as little as 7 per cent of the meaning that gets taken from what we say comes from the words we use.

→ Our non-verbal behaviour and the tone and rhythm of our voice make up the other 93 per cent and so are really important.

→ Non-verbal behaviour includes eye contact, the gestures that we make, the facial expressions that we have, our positioning relative to the person we are talking to and our posture relative to the person we are talking to.

→ Making eye contact is a very powerful way of connecting to a child.

→ Children are more likely to do what you do rather than do what you say, so always remember to be a good role-model.

→ Make sure to show your child that you are listening to them by turning to face them, coming down to their level and looking them in the eye.

→ Use the same down-to-their-level positioning and eye contact when you want to give a direction to your child and you want to be sure that they have heard. Shouting from the kitchen is a mug's game.

→ How your voice sounds when you talk includes things like your tone of voice, the rhythm of your speech and the loudness of your speech.

→ If you want to calm a situation down you must ensure that your voice sounds calm too.

→ Show your child that you are listening by being active in this role.

→ Active listening means focusing your attention on your child, repeating what you hear, reflecting what you see and summarizing what gets said.

→ Encouraging conversation requires you to ask open questions. Smiling and nodding are a good help too.

2
PROMOTING CHILDREN'S PLAY

FUN AND GAMES ARE ALL IN A DAY'S WORK FOR YOUR CHILD

Children use play for lots of things. They explore their world through play. They communicate feelings through play. They work through stressful situations and relieve tension through play and they also use it as an opportunity to spend time and develop connections with the people they care about. Most parents, though, aim to get their children into independent play as quickly as possible. We forget, or don't realize in the first place, that we are important people in our children's lives and so we are an important part of their world and therefore their play. How many of us use our children's playtime as an opportunity to tackle a myriad of other household tasks? In this chapter I want to help you think about play as part of the bigger picture of children's development, and a crucial part of your relationship with your child.

THE PURPOSE OF PLAY

All of children's play is an opportunity for learning, growth and development. For example, water play in the sink or in the bath is a time to learn about the volume, the movement and the properties of water, and the physical characteristics of small pots, big pots, jars, straws and whatever else happens to be in the sink.

How do you know now that when you pour water from a big pot into a little pot it doesn't all fit in? You probably learned it as a child when you poured it, and it began to overflow the edges. How did you learn to balance a full cup of water? Probably from playing as a child. How did you learn, like Archimedes, that an object will displace its own volume of water? You may have learned the name Archimedes from a text book or from somebody telling you but you experienced it through play. Having had the experience

Play is an opportunity to get into your child's world in a unique interactive way

through play, you then knew that what you were being taught was true. So, when children play, they are experiencing their world. It is up to us as adults to help them to categorize, understand and make sense of those experiences. But if we are not letting them play and we are not with them when they play, then we are missing out on those opportunities.

Play is an opportunity to get into your child's world in a unique interactive way. Because children will use play to try to make sense of the world they live in, playing with them connects you to their world even more strongly. You can relate to your child sometimes with more freedom and certainly with more confidence when you play with them regularly. Playing with your child is a fast track to a good relationship. Having a good relationship is a central building block to managing them and their behaviour down through the years.

The goals of play for you as a parent are:

☆ To have fun with your child

☆ To enter into their world and see things from their perspective

☆ To build up a positive relationship with your child

☆ To share in their learning

☆ To balance up all the time where you have to be in charge and setting limits with some time where your child gets to be in charge.

**The goals of play for your pre-school child
(even though they could never consciously know this) are:**

☆ To have fun

☆ To explore their world and scale it down to manageable sizes

☆ To express often complex or difficult feelings that they either can't verbalize or don't want to verbalize

☆ To experiment and learn about all aspects of life

☆ To practise turn-taking, sharing and building relationships with peers.

The value of play for children, and small children especially, should never be underestimated. Having the space, time and tools to play are critical needs for your child's social, emotional and physical development. In this chapter I will look at different ways to play with children.

PLAYING WITH BABIES

Babies don't really need toys. What they need is lots of your time, your attention and the opportunities to experience the world. The world gives huge amounts of those opportunities through different tastes, smells, textures, sounds and sights. As your baby grows and develops so too will all their senses. They don't need any special toys, for example, to help them develop those senses. Some toy manufacturers would have you believe that their particular product will engage your baby and promote, for example, their developing eyesight, because of the contrasting colours and shapes it has. So too will exposing your baby to all the sights, colours, light and shade of your own home and the larger world outside. When babies do explore their world around them they tend to do it using all of their senses. That's why you will often see your baby looking at something, picking it up and handling it and then popping it in their mouth to check out the taste and the texture.

Babies don't really need toys. What they need is lots of your time, your attention and the opportunities to experience the world

When babies arrive, particularly first babies, we often think of them as helpless, receptive little mites. We, their parents, keep giving (food, warmth, love, clothes, clean nappies, time and attention) while all they seem to be able to do is just lie there receiving. However, the reality is that from day one babies are interactive rather than simply reactive. Babies will make sounds, movements and facial expressions that are all designed to establish a connection to us their parents and caregivers. For babies, this is both an instinctual and survival imperative but it also becomes playing.

When babies are having their nappy changed is a common time when we instinctively attempt to play with them. Think of all those times when you held your baby's feet and made little pedalling movements with their legs or stretched their arms out or stroked their tummies or blew with a farting noise on their skin. In our house we call that a flarple. I bet that nappy-changing time was also the first time when you played the game of peek-a-boo with your child.

Hopefully, one of the things that you will have noticed while you are doing these things with your baby is that you begin to take turns with them. So, for example, you might move their arms and then stop and wait to see their reaction. Do they smile? Do they look serious? Do they cry? Usually they smile, and that reaction then tells

From day one babies are interactive rather than simply reactive

you that it's OK for you to do it again. That action by you / response from your baby / repeated action from you sequence is the beginnings of conversation. It is just as likely too that your baby will begin the sequence by making some action, movement or sound. Those are the moments to be ready to react to them.

So there in the midst of playing with your baby you are teaching them a hugely important life skill: turn-taking.

When babies make sounds we often copy them. This also becomes a game and it's also part of their learning and development. When we play and chat with babies, it's interesting to note how our voice changes. Most of us adopt a higher pitch and a sing-song cadence. This is hard to demonstrate in a book. But when you talk to your baby you will know what I mean.

PHYSICAL PLAY WITH BABIES

When your tiny baby arrives home you can often feel that holding them and touching them is like handling the finest bone china. You can be anxious that, if you handle them wrong, somehow you will break them. The reality is that babies are a lot more robust than we give them credit for. Certainly in the early weeks it's important to support their head and for the first few months it's advisable not to let them carry weight vertically on their spine. Beyond that, however, there is nothing to stop you playfully interacting with your baby by moving all of their limbs and maybe rocking their body from side to side. This is good both for their physical development and also to give them a tangible experience that their limbs are connected to them.

As your baby grows older and bigger and stronger, you are going to find lots of different ways that they like to be held, rocked, rolled, tumbled as well as cuddled. A general rule of thumb is that, if your baby is chuckling or giggling, then they are enjoying the experience. Sometimes a bit of physical play like this can be just the distraction that a fretful baby needs, although sometimes it won't. Basically, the message is, don't be afraid to hold, touch and horseplay gently with your baby. If they don't like it they will let you know quickly enough.

There is nothing to stop you playfully interacting with your baby by moving all of their limbs and maybe rocking their body from side to side

PLAYING WITH SMALL CHILDREN

When small children are playing, they are really trying to explore their world and make sense of it. As a result they love repetition, trial and error and re-enacting real-life situations. As a parent, watching this, you can often be tempted to get stuck in with them and to show them how it should be done. I would encourage you absolutely to follow your urge to get stuck in but to resist your urge to show them how it should be done. Playing with children should happen at their pace and according to their rules. The only exception to this is where those rules make it dangerous for somebody else or themselves. When children remain in charge of their play, it meets their needs and not ours.

You can imagine a typical scene, where a child is building something from blocks. A father comes along and says, 'Oh, what are you doing?' His daughter looks up and replies with a big smile on her face, 'Making a house.' Dad then plonks himself down, takes a load of blocks and starts to build a real house. It will then go either of two ways. Her dad will build himself a fine house using up all the available blocks including a few key pieces that she has in her pile. Alternatively, her dad will painstakingly reconstruct her 'house' so that it actually looks like a house. His daughter's reaction could be anything. She might be pleased that she has a new house to look at. She might be pleased that her dad even took the time to spend with her. She might equally be frustrated, however, that she wasn't left to build as she had wanted. She might be frustrated that all the blocks have been used up. She might have decided that she can't build a house now because her attempt looks a little bit feeble compared to her father's and so she feels like a failure. She could also end up frustrated because the playtime she thought she would have with her father has been spent simply observing him.

> **Playing with children should happen at their pace and according to their rules. The only exception to this is where those rules make it dangerous**

In that situation it would have been ideal if her dad had followed her lead. What that means is doing things according to the way his daughter wants rather than the way he wants. In this situation, when the dad came over and asked, 'What are you doing?' he should have followed it up with a range of other questions. So we will assume that his daughter replied, 'Making a house.' A good question then to ask is 'What kind of house?' Another good question is 'Would you like me to help you?' Depending on the answer, you may then want to ask, 'Can I watch you?' We can assume at this stage that the dad has been given an invitation to join his daughter in her play. Following her lead then becomes a process of constantly checking with her what she is doing and either offering to join in and assist with that or doing something that helps her achieve what she wants.

PARALLEL PLAY

Another important thing to remember when you are playing with toddlers is that toddlers like to engage in what's known as 'parallel play'. This means that they like to play alongside somebody else but not necessarily interacting with them. This is simply a developmental phase. In the example above the three-year-old daughter might have preferred it if her dad built his own house with blocks rather than trying to help her build her house and using what she perceived as 'her blocks'.

When you get a group of toddlers together it can be really amusing to see them all play, but none of them playing with each other. Sometimes they will play with each other but more often than not it ends up in a fight or a struggle over a particular toy. This is the age when you know that it's good for your child to have social interaction with other toddlers even though it's very hard work for you because you are constantly intervening to help them sort out their differences. It is important to remember, however, not to try to force them to play with other children at this age or to try to force them to play with you. If you do, your child will feel possibly anxious and probably frustrated and they are highly likely to act both of those feelings out by becoming bold or disruptive.

Sharing and playing cooperatively are skills that need a little bit of encouragement and lots of reinforcement

PROMOTING AND ENCOURAGING SHARING

When you have got a group of children, the single most satisfying thing to see is them all taking turns in sharing toys. It makes for a relaxed playtime, where you can begin to take time for yourself, either to do other stuff around the house or even read a book or the newspaper. However, sharing and playing cooperatively are skills that need a little bit of encouragement and lots of reinforcement from a parent or adult. Your two-year-old, for example, is going to really struggle to share their toys with any other child, or even with you. Part of their struggle is their belief that every toy belongs to them and them alone.

Two-year-olds become very proprietorial about things. This means that getting them to share or to take turns requires lots and lots of patience. It will have helped if, as a baby, they played lots of turn-taking games. This means that they know and can rely upon the fact that they will get their turn and that you or another child will take their turn and won't extend it unfairly.

> **If you ever spot your child sharing or taking turns, then make sure you praise this behaviour**

Of course, when your two-year-old is with a child of the same age, then it's highly likely that that child will not be able to take a fair turn, so adult intervention is required. When you intervene, you need to tell your child about sharing and that sharing is a good thing, that it's a value that you believe in, and that you like it when your child shares. So in real life you would be saying things to your child like: 'Now, Paul, you give one of those balls to Ben, and then Ben can roll it back to you. Remember, we always share our toys in this house. If you roll the ball to Ben, I'll help Ben roll it back to you. I really like it when I see you sharing your toys.'

If you remember what we talked about in terms of the communication earlier, then this is a time to keep your tone of voice light, encouraging and easy-going. If you begin to sound controlling, demanding or insistent, it's quite likely that your child will react in response to your attempts to control them by becoming obstinate rather than softening in response to your attempts to be encouraging. In an ideal world, there would be other balls around so that you can demonstrate what you would like your child to do when playing with Ben, so you can take another ball, roll it to Ben and then have Ben roll it back to you. This then shows your own child exactly what it is that is expected of them and makes it much more likely that they will perceive this game as fun rather than as the potential for the loss of their ball.

Of course, if you ever spot your child sharing or taking turns, then make sure you praise this behaviour. As with any kind of praise be specific with your child about what it is that you like to see them do.

A typical praise might be: 'Paul, you shared your ball with Ben, now the two of you can have lots of fun together. Well done.' So in your phrase you have named the

> You need to tell your child about sharing and that sharing is a good thing, that it's a value that you believe in, and that you like it when your child shares

behaviour that you liked (the sharing) and the benefits of that behaviour (the fun the children can have together) and you have let them know that this has pleased you as their parent (the comment about doing well).

It's also important that you role-model sharing behaviour if you want to see your child also sharing. It would be hypocritical to expect your child to share if you find it hard to share as well. Even though we think we all share very easily I would guess that there are probably lots of times when actually you show your child that you don't want to share either. An example would be when you are writing, and your child asks whether they can take a turn with your pen. Most of us will send them off to their colouring bag to take out their own crayons or pencils. Usually, we will justify it because we are too busy, and what we are writing has to be done quickly, and that if we don't get it finished now we won't get it finished at all. Or what about those times when we are cooking, and our child pulls over their chair, climbs up and asks to stir, mix, chop, peel and otherwise 'help'. Our reaction often depends on our mood and can easily be a sharp refusal because either it's too dangerous, or it's too busy a time, or the task is too delicate. Even though we will justify the refusal to our child, we are still giving them a message that we struggle to share.

I have often found myself in a situation where I am cleaning my car (to my own internally held standard!), and my children want to take a turn with the hose or with the sponge, and I have to swallow hard to keep from saying no. The last thing I want, usually, is smears of dirty water all down the side of my car. However, I struggle to tell myself that this is simply my impatience and my need for perfection and it doesn't meet the needs of my children, especially as I know in years to come I will probably be asking my children to clean my car as part of their chores. I can hardly expect them to do it if for years I have refused to let them share the task and help. And, even though I know that refusing their offer of help isn't a good idea either in the short or the long term, there are still times when I do refuse their help simply because I have my own agenda and my own needs. So, despite knowing what might be a better route to follow, we all have to acknowledge that sometimes we are going to make a complete mess of things, repeatedly.

Two-year-olds become very proprietorial about things. This means that getting them to share or take turns requires lots and lots of patience

OBSERVATIONAL COMMENTARY

Whenever you play with your child, or even if you are not playing but just interacting with them, it's a good idea to make a commentary on what you see them doing. I call this observational commentary. In order to make a commentary on what you see them doing you have to be observing them, which means you must be noticing them. This point is not lost on your toddler. Toddlers love to be noticed. So every opportunity you get to show them that they are being noticed means that they have less need to come looking for, or demanding, your attention at other times.

Imagine a scene where your child is 'helping' you to do the washing-up. As they do their little bit beside you, you might be saying things like: 'Oh, you are using the sponge to clean that cup. Now you are pouring water over the cup to take all the suds off. Look, the cup is sitting on the draining board. Now all the water is dripping off it. That's a plate you are cleaning now. You are wiping the sponge round and round and round. Oh look, when you squeeze the sponge lots of sudsy water drips off. Uh oh, oh dear, you are dripping it on to the counter-top. Let's use a cloth to wipe that up. Ah, you are doing a great job wiping with the cloth. Now you are back with the sponge and the plate. Oh, you are trying to balance the plate on the draining board, and it's wobbling. I will help you keep it upright, now, there it is standing beside the cup.' And of course this kind of commentary can go on for as long as the washing-up takes.

> **Toddlers love to be noticed. So every opportunity you get to show them that they are being noticed means that they have less need to come looking for, or demanding, your attention at other times**

Not only are you showing your child that you are noticing them, which they will love, but you are also helping them develop their language. By naming all of their behaviours and all of the objects they are coming into contact with you are expanding their vocabulary. You are helping them with what's called their 'receptive language'. This is your child's ability to understand what's said to them. Commentary like this helps receptive language because it links the words directly with the actions or with the objects in real time. So what your child gets is the actual experience that they are having matched with language that describes it. This kind of commentary is great for any child but is especially good for a child whose language is slower to develop.

When you first start commenting on your child's behaviour like this, it can seem a little forced and a little obvious. It may not feel very natural. But if you practise it, it soon becomes natural. Your child won't ever have an issue with it. They will be delighted to be noticed in such a concrete way. This will be a very tangible experience for them of being attended to and of having 100 per cent of your notice. Such attention is a luxury for any child. Some parents believe that, by giving this kind of concentrated attention, they will

Paradoxically, the more concentrated attention you give your child the less they will demand it at other times

be setting their child up to expect it all the time, knowing that they can't deliver that intensity of attention all the time. Paradoxically, though, the more attention like this that you give your child the less they will demand it at other times. In fact, what is happening is that a lot of their needs for attention are being met in those concentrated interactions, and so they don't need to come looking for attention to the same extent. It is akin to letting your child have a big, long drink of water when they are thirsty rather than limiting the amount they can drink such that they keep coming back to you demanding more and more water. Like our need for water, our need for attention can be satisfied for longer periods by getting a good quenching every so often.

PHYSICAL PLAY WITH CHILDREN

It's amazing, sometimes, how cautious we remain about physically playing with children, even after they have moved from babyhood. Sometimes we hold back because we are afraid of hurting children. Other times we hold back because we are afraid we might look silly playing a chasing game, for example. Children, however, love it when adults play physically with them. They love to be chased, they love to be caught, they love to be tumbled to the ground, they love to be wrestled and they love to feel that there is someone bigger, stronger and faster than them that they can both challenge and occasionally overcome in a safe way.

The concept of safety is important, especially the emotional safety of the experience. Physical play shouldn't result in your child getting anxious or overwhelmed. Children need to know that your intention is to play, not to hurt or belittle or demean them. If you are play-fighting, for example, then there may be times that you win and times that you let them win. The winner doesn't gloat, or put down the efforts of the loser. You have the responsibility for managing the safety of the physical and emotional environment for this kind of play.

> When you chase a child, part of what they want is to be caught and part of what they want is to continue to stay ahead of you

Because you are the adult, you have to be aware of any potential dangers in the surroundings that might affect you or your child. For example, if you are going to play chasing, make sure there are no obvious hazards for you or them to trip over. The architect who designed our house must have been a child at heart. Our house is designed so that the sitting room, kitchen, eating area, hallway and bedrooms all interconnect on a single floor. As a result our children and their friends spend huge proportions of their time running in great big circles around the house.

Try as we might, there are invariably trips, falls and bumps along the way. But we do try to reduce the danger. For example, we move the kitchen table so that a child careering from the sitting room into the kitchen won't easily bang into it. Similarly, our children's bedroom floor is often strewn with toys, and if we see them chasing each other we usually try to stop them until they have at least tidied a clear route through the room.

When you chase a child, part of what they want is to be caught and part of what they want is to continue to stay ahead of you. The inevitability of being caught is apparent, because you are bigger and faster. However, for the child, as part of their own developing self-confidence and belief in their own ability, they need to feel that there is always a chance that they will outrun you. You will notice, however, if you do chase your children, that if you deliberately hold back and don't catch them, sooner or later they will stop almost to

Physical play shouldn't result in your child getting anxious or overwhelmed. Children need to know that your intention is to play, not to hurt or belittle or demean them

invite you to catch up and grab hold of them. I believe this is because for the child it makes sense for you to catch them. It doesn't make sense for them to be able to escape. However, you can use your apparent inability to catch them as a way of bolstering their self-esteem. As you chase your four-year-old around and come to a huffing, puffing stop, you can call out after them, 'Wow, you've gotten so big I can't keep up with you.' It may sound obvious, and I believe a lot of us do it naturally, but it's also good to remember that it's serving a purpose as well as being a bit of fun.

The other kind of physical play is termed in America rough-housing and over here

is more usually known as horseplay. In our house, it has a number of names: 'tumble time', 'dinosaur fighting', 'rolly-tumbly-monster' and probably other names that my children have yet to invent. A bit of wrestling, or play-fighting, is a great way to help children burn off excess energy. It also allows them to experiment with their own physical strength, agility and self-belief. Sometimes it can also allow your child to work off some feelings, especially anger or frustration, that they have been carrying.

Again, because you are the adult, you need to take responsibility for ensuring the safety of the area in which you are going to have your play-fight. You also need to set up some rules with your child to ensure that nobody gets deliberately hurt. The rules that I would commonly use are:

 No deliberate hurting

 No kicking or punching

If anybody says stop then the game stops immediately.

I think horseplay like this between a parent and a child is both good fun and also potentially therapeutic where there are problems in the relationship. Children often carry huge amounts of frustration, and, as we know, toddlers are not often best able to communicate verbally that they are having problems. So when you see them beginning to act out their frustrations in other ways it can be a great idea to distract and divert them into some horseplay.

What you often find is that within the comparative safety and confines of the game they can express a huge amount of their physical anger in wrestling with you. You can even encourage this. You can suggest to them as you're rolling around on the bed or on the floor with them that they imagine they are fighting a big 'frustration monster'. You can suggest that they need to use all their strength in order to beat the frustration.

You can suggest to them as you're rolling around on the bed or on the floor with them that they imagine they are fighting a big 'frustration monster'

You can encourage them to be as angry as they like with the frustration monster. My own children, when I've tried this, have lapped it up. You can often see the fury etched in their face as their cheeks go red with their exertion to try and pin you down, roll you over or just generally push against the strength that you have.

What I am describing is another way of children pushing the limits. However, in a game like this, the limits are very defined, and the boundaries are the safety that you provide by being able to hold, push and roll them. If you struggle to hold limits in other areas then this can be a good way to show your child that you can hold them and, as a consequence, the limit.

Of course like everything there is a time and a place when physical play is best. Certainly, just before bed is not a great time for horseplay with your child. Horseplay, by its nature, gets the blood pumping and excites and stimulates your child. This is rarely the intention of a good bedtime routine!

A bit of wrestling, or play-fighting, is a great way to help children to burn off excess energy. It also allows them to experiment with their own physical strength, agility and self-belief

SIBLINGS NOT PLAYING TOGETHER: THE TRICKY PROBLEM OF SIBLING RIVALRY

Usually the kinds of problems that parents talk to me about are when their children don't get on with each other rather than when they do. You will hear lots of different stories from different parents about how having children close together in age means that they are more of a friend for each other and have more in common and so will get on better. Others will argue that spacing children apart and leaving a longer gap of maybe three to four years between each child allows the children to have different interests so that they don't compete or fight over the same things at the same time. Who knows, maybe the answer lies somewhere in between. What's always true, however, is that you need to take the temperament of each individual child into consideration when you are trying to understand why children do and don't get on. Just because you are in the same family doesn't mean that you have to like or get on with your brothers and sisters.

If you have children who are constantly fighting and between whom there seems to be a constant rivalry there are things you can do. In the first instance, though, it is great to be able to minimize jealousy from the start.

INTRODUCING A NEW BABY

Parents often wonder how best to introduce the notion of a new arrival to the family with an older sibling. So, for example, how do you tell your three-year-old that there is going to be a new baby coming who is going to take up a huge amount of your time and attention, not because they are being horrible but just because they need it? However it's introduced it's always a change for the older child. Sometimes they can be delighted in anticipating that change and then be a bit shocked when it actually happens. Equally, they can be really upset in anticipating the change but actually cope fine when the new baby comes. Sometimes it's hard to predict. There are things that you can do, however, that should make the transition easier for an older brother or sister.

Generally, I believe, it's a good idea to tell an older brother or sister that a new baby is expected as soon as you begin to tell the wider public. It would be much better for your three-year-old to hear it from you directly that a baby sister or brother is expected than to hear it at third hand from an uncle, aunt, granny or grandad. It's also a good idea to tell them accurately what's happening. Try to explain that the baby is growing inside your tummy in a special place called a womb. Try to explain that the growing takes a long time and that as the baby grows your tummy will get bigger and rounder. Be prepared for sporadic questions over the next number of weeks and months as your child tries to create a context for this new information.

It's a good idea to tell an older brother or sister that a new baby is expected as soon as you begin to tell the wider public

You can also involve and engage your child in the pregnancy in other ways. For example, if you are attending antenatal clinics, it may be possible for your child to accompany you so that they can hear the tracing of the baby's heartbeat or even see the scan of the baby.

You can get lots of books that tell stories about the arrival of new babies into a household and how this causes a huge distraction for parents and seems to leave little time for an older child. These kinds of stories also explain that this lessening of attention is not intentional, is short lived and in fact reflects a maturity on the older child's part to be able to cope. They also usually all end with a parent making special time for the older child. Knowing that this is likely to be the experience when their baby brother or sister arrives may be comforting.

You can also give your child a sense of shared responsibility in the preparations for the arrival of the baby by including them in some of the decisions that have to be made. For example, you might be trying to decide where the new baby will sleep, which brand of nappies it will use, where you will set up the baby-changing table or mat and other such practical, albeit trivial, decisions. It may be the case that the older sibling can make some of those decisions with you. You may also want to let your child help to choose a name for its brother or sister. I will warn you, however, that sometimes the names that are suggested are so outlandish or awful that you may end up disappointing the older brother or sister more by having to say no constantly to their generous and thoughtful name suggestions.

When the baby does finally arrive, it's great if it can bring a small gift for the older brother or sister as a little way of saying, 'Hi, thanks for letting me be your little brother or sister.' Even when the baby does bring home a present, jealousy can quickly emerge, and you may need to spend time really trying to help your older child understand that, yes, they do feel put out, yes, they do feel like they are not having the same amount of your time and attention and yes, that is a pretty miserable place to be. Despite all of those upsetting feelings there will be times when you can't give your attention to your older child or when you do understand that they are missing out and so you are going to deliberately try and make special time for them.

You may also want to include them in some of the daily tasks and routines with their little brother or sister. For example, they may want to help run a bath, get the nappies from the changing bag, line up the baby wipes or cotton wool, choose the vests or baby-gros or pat their little brother or sister on the back to help the wind come up. Including your child in this way gives them a sense of shared ownership of the new baby and also helps them develop a sense of responsibility and caring rather than just jealousy.

> When the baby does finally arrive, it's great if it can bring a small gift for the older brother or sister as a little way of saying, 'Hi, thanks for letting me be your little brother or sister'

DEALING WITH SIBLING RIVALRY

Let's assume you did your best to soften the arrival of a new sister or brother. Despite your best attempts, your two children fight all the time. They can't share toys without a row and they can't seem to even sit on the same sofa watching TV without somebody getting a thump.

Sibling rivalry is a real phenomenon, and there are books written just dealing with it alone. In the first instance it is worth taking a look at how you divide your time and attention between your children. Even if you believe you are scrupulously fair in dividing your time, you may find that your children have a different view. A belief, amongst siblings, that you favour one over the other runs deeply and painfully. If you find that you are more often giving out to one child for causing the rows or fights, then you can guess that they are feeling left out somewhere in the attention hierarchy.

If you give your children a joint task to do, where they will get equal rewards for achieving it together, you may find that suddenly they can learn to get on

If you give your children a joint task to do, where they will get equal rewards for achieving it together, you may find that they can learn to get on. For example, getting your six- and four-year-olds to tidy their toys together, with your help if needed, can be a real boost to them when you can praise them. You can also reward them in this situation with some extra privilege for working together. In this instance you are praising or rewarding not just their achievement of a clean floor but also the fact that they worked together. If you were helping them, then you can bolster their togetherness as they work and help by intervening early if disagreements arise.

If your children do play together well for a while before things disintegrate into a row, then it can help to be part of their play for some time each day. That way, you can praise them when you see them playing well and teach them negotiating skills when things get more tense.

Sometimes sibling rivalry can be helped by identifying for each child what their individual and unique strengths are. This gives them a sense of self that is separate from their sibling and so they no longer need feel rivals.

TOYS FOR PLAY

When you have your first baby no one really tells you about the fact that you are going to need extra space, not for the child, but for the number of toys they are going to collect over their lifetime. While there are lots of good toys out there, there is also a huge amount of junk. I would guess that most families, unless they have remarkable powers of avoidance, have gathered vast quantities of junk toys by the time their child is six. It's interesting to note, as well, that children don't seem to need a huge range of toys available to them. Often they will pick one or two toys that they will play with over and over again.

The tools of play can be quite basic. Household objects form the basis for a huge amount of play for a pre-school child. Toys are great, but your child doesn't need lots of shiny plastic and electronic noises to stimulate and engage them. A pot and a wooden spoon, for example, will keep an 18–24-month-old busy for ages, cooking, mixing, filling, emptying, banging, creating. Their head will be full of imaginary tasks and goals. As they create their own world from the objects around them they let their imaginations fly. This is a good thing.

Toys are great, but your child doesn't need lots of shiny plastic and electronic noises to stimulate and engage them

So what are the best toys for children to have? In my view, the best toys are toys that allow your child to express their individuality and their imagination and to re-enact their experiences of the world around them. As my own children have grown and developed over the years I have watched them play a lot. I like to think that they are pretty representative of most children and so the choices they make about toys are, I would imagine, also pretty representative.

Dolls and doll's houses are always a source of huge attraction to children, girls and boys alike. Doll's houses offer children the chance to recreate the world as they would like it. Suddenly the bathroom can be downstairs, the kitchen can be upstairs, the bedroom can be non-existent, and everyone can live on top of everyone else. There is also the opportunity to replay experiences that they have had themselves using the figures or locations of the house. In their play they may create new endings to old events, and this means that they are sorting things out and creating a context for what they have experienced and then moving on.

Other really good toys to have are building blocks, cars, tractors, human figures, animal figures and so on. I like toys that allow a child to construct and create and use their imagination. In this way they will tell you about the important things that are going on for them at the moment. For example, if a child builds a tower of blocks and then immediately knocks it down, they may be reflecting their belief that the world is an unpredictable place, and nothing is ever safe. They could also just like the sound and sight of crashing blocks! A child building a fortress out of the same blocks that cannot be knocked down by invading forces may be saying something about how they perceive their world to be safe and secure and stable.

Action figures – human, humanoid or animal – allow a child to re-enact scenes from their lives, either as things are or as they would like things to be. They can make sense of experiences they have themselves or experiences they witness by playing the same scenarios and twisting the ending or getting the play figures to experience feelings that they themselves may not experience.

Computer games and video games are unnecessary and bad for children of this age. In my view, even TV viewing is detrimental to the development of pre-schoolers. All too often we use the TV and video games as 'babysitters' for our children. There is no doubt that TV and video games are engaging, and children love to watch and play. Evidence from research suggests, however, that children who watch lots of television do less well academically and are at greater risk of things like obesity and type 2 diabetes.

Television usually shows a fantasy or make-believe world (especially cartoons), but small children are not well able to distinguish between the fantasy they view and

> Computer games and video games are unnecessary and bad for children of this age. All too often we use the TV and video games as 'babysitters' for our children

reality. This presents real dangers for children. One mother showed me the scar on her four-year-old's tummy after he launched himself from the garden gate pillar, like his superhero. Unfortunately he didn't realize that he wasn't going to fly like his hero and so he fell and caught himself against the gate on the way down.

There is no experiential component to TV watching or video-gaming. The images don't allow children to engage beyond their senses of sight and hearing. TV lets children opt out of their world rather than engage in it. Their brains are stimulated while watching television, possibly over-stimulated, and yet there is no physical component to balance it. Most children watching television will be lethargic while viewing, and so there is this dissonance between their brain activity and their body activity.

If you do choose to let your child watch TV or play video games, then I would encourage you to be vigilant and to monitor and restrict what they view or play and how much they view and play. Even cartoon channels on TV contain advertising, and if you don't monitor their exposure to that advertising you do not know how they are being influenced, potentially in opposite ways to those you believe are right. Up to the age of six children are not aware that a central purpose of advertising is to influence them, and so their innocence and naivety can be exploited. Children's advertising often promotes unhealthy lifestyles and it increases the demands that your children subsequently place on you for an ever-expanding range of 'things'.

TV lets children opt out of their world rather than engage in it

Think, too, about how much of your family time is spent watching television. Frequently you are in one room watching TV, and your child is in another. In this scenario there is no opportunity to develop the relationships that are so central to managing, guiding and teaching your children. If children watch too much TV, there is no time to play, and play is central to the development of children.

KEY POINTS TO REMEMBER

Babies like, and need, to be played with.

Even if babies seem to be simply receptive they are not, and play allows them to develop important skills like turn-taking and generally stimulates their development.

Playing with small children needs to happen at their pace and be led by them; be involved in the play but don't direct it.

Sharing doesn't come naturally and needs to be encouraged by reinforcing any sharing that does occur and by role-modelling how to share and take turns.

Using observational commentary while you play helps to develop children's receptive language and to give them a powerful feeling of being attended to and noticed.

Don't be afraid to be physical in play with babies and small children; they love to be challenged and to challenge in a safe environment, and it can be a great way to help them to burn off energy and frustration.

Sibling rivalry is very common, and you can sometimes reduce its impact by helping to prepare your older child for the birth of a sibling.

Sometimes rivalry continues because your children perceive some unfairness in the division of your time and attention.

Getting children to work together to achieve a task that they are rewarded for equally can be a good way to get them to play better together.

Some toys are overrated, and the best kinds of toys for children are those that stimulate their imaginations.

TV and video games are bad for children, especially if they are unlimited.

3

RECOGNIZING FEELINGS

THE HEART AND SOUL OF UNDERSTANDING BEHAVIOUR

Small children experience strong feelings. Just like an adult they can feel frustrated, angry, happy, upset, sad, jealous, delighted, hopeless – pretty much any feeling you can imagine. But what is different about their experience of those feelings is their ability to express them appropriately. Most tantrums are an expression of feeling (often frustration) and as such they are valid; they are just not the most appropriate way of communicating the feeling. Don't forget, though, that while we may feel it is not appropriate it is highly effective. Think back to what we know about communication. In normal conversation 93 per cent of the meaning we'll take comes from their non-verbal behaviour and tone of voice. A crying, foot-stomping child is simply expecting 100 per cent of the meaning to be understood.

We often overlook or fail to understand the importance of supporting the emotional development of small children. How many times, for example, are children excluded from things like family funerals (even of close family relatives) because 'they might be upset'? I reckon it is better to let children feel the feelings (even really powerful feelings like upset or anger) and then help them to understand and develop a context for those feelings. In my experience of working with children a significant majority of the difficulties that parents present their children with are due to their child having a range of feelings that they haven't been able to express or can't express in an appropriate way.

We could expect an adult to be able to say when they feel tired or grumpy, or if they feel upset and angry with someone else. But even with adults we rarely get just the words describing their feelings. Adults have their own forms of tantrums. We are just as likely sometimes to scream, stamp our feet, slam doors and storm off. Despite our own inability to 'appropriately' express our feelings, we still have high expectations of our small children.

The reasons for non-expression of feelings vary. Some children don't have the language (because they are too young); others feel it is not OK (that they will cause greater upset to their parents, for example); others deny the feelings they have (because they are too painful or they believe someone else will refute their feelings). Parents have a role in teaching children the language of feelings and in encouraging the expression of those feelings in words as well as actions. Obviously, we are trying to teach them to develop appropriate ways of dealing with those feelings – vital for managing those temper tantrums!

Before we even get stuck into helping children cope with their feelings, we need to be coping with our own feelings. If we are not calm in responding to our children, then it is very difficult, if not impossible, to be able to understand their distress or anger because we are blinded by our own. This involves two processes: reducing our overall stress so that we can be calmer and then managing our feelings in the moment.

THIS CHAPTER LOOKS AT ...

Emotional intelligence and why it is worth investing in the promotion of emotionally healthy and expressive children

Dealing with stress

Understanding and managing your own feelings

Empathy – what does it mean and how do you show it

What is your child feeling? Understanding the feelings at typical family flashpoints (getting dressed, getting out the door, going to bed and so on)

Doing emotional support

EMOTIONAL INTELLIGENCE

Emotional intelligence, often measured as an emotional quotient, or EQ, might be even more important than general intelligence, measured as an intelligence quotient, or IQ. Emotions are an essential tool for having a successful and fulfilling life. Our emotions will affect our relationships with other people or our self-identity and self-esteem and our ability to complete a task. Theorists and researchers make links between having a high EQ and future success in life and business. Practically, what they mean is that we need to stay in control of our emotions so that they work for us rather than work against us.

Emotional intelligence theory, as put forward by Daniel Goleman, suggests that there are five main elements to emotional intelligence. They are:

Knowing your own emotions. This really is a self-awareness to be able to recognize your feelings as they are happening. It's really important to be able to read our true emotions because, unless we know what they are and when we are feeling them, we can't remain in charge of them.

⭐ **Managing emotions.** Once we have that awareness of what we are feeling we need to be able to manage it. Managing it means not acting out our frustrations, but rather finding ways to comfort ourselves. Managing feelings means dealing with things like anxiety so it doesn't prevent us from achieving things. In life we are going to be faced with a range of different emotions in response to the experiences that we have and in order to be able to recover from life's setbacks and upsets we need to be able to stay in charge of those feelings.

⭐ **Motivating oneself.** We need to be able to use our emotions to lead us in the direction of our goals. This sometimes means delaying gratification and holding back from being impulsive. This kind of emotional self-control allows us to stay focused on, and attentive to, what it is that we want to achieve.

⭐ **Recognizing feelings in others.** Being attuned to the subtle social signals that indicate what others need or want is a really important skill to have. It is really the extension of self-awareness to the awareness of others. Being able to put yourself into somebody else's shoes means that you are more likely to tailor your behaviour to outcomes that will work for you and for them. This ability to recognize the feelings of others is called empathy.

⭐ **Managing relationships.** This is where emotional intelligence can really benefit us in the longer term. Managing relationships is really about trying to manage the emotions of other people. It's a skill that great leaders have to be able to motivate, encourage and support other people. It will also allow us to get on with a wide range of people, even if we don't like them!

I want you to be better able to understand the feelings of your children to set in place the building blocks for them to develop their emotional intelligence. If you can show an awareness of your child's emotions, and you can then teach them what that feeling is, then you are sowing the seeds of their own self-awareness and the ability to manage their emotions.

Researchers have demonstrated that children who have been 'emotionally coached' like this by their parents have better physical health and score higher academically than children whose parents don't offer such emotional guidance. These children get along better with friends; they have fewer behaviour problems; and they generally experience fewer negative feelings and more positive feelings.

By focusing on their feelings you are creating emotionally intelligent children, and emotionally intelligent children are more resilient. So, while an emotionally intelligent child will still experience sadness, anger or fear under difficult circumstances, they will be better able to cope with this distress and to comfort themselves and to bounce back. Being emotionally aware like this is a proven buffer for children against the impact of lots of life's troubles.

Normally I am not a person to think too far ahead in planning my child's life. I don't spend a huge amount of time defining what their aspirations should be or preparing them for a particular role in life. I like to let my children just be, to experience, grow, learn and develop at their own pace. Working with their emotions, however, is the one area where I deliberately invest energy in order to give them that solid basis for the development of their emotional intelligence. It's my belief – and research backs it up – that if children are emotionally literate and intelligent then they will be able to cope flexibly and confidently with whatever life throws their way. So whether my children are successful or unsuccessful with tasks, activities, sports or studies, I can know that they have the internal capacity to cope. This means that I can encourage them to experience lots of different things and rely on them to know what's good and bad for them.

I know, however, that I can't help my children with their emotions unless I have a good handle on my own emotions. In my experience, the times when parents don't understand and manage their own feelings are when they are stressed. Dealing with stress, therefore, sets us up to be emotionally better connected to our children because we are better connected to our own emotions.

DEALING WITH STRESS

Being with children can be a very stressful and hazardous occupation. The demands that they place on your time and on your energy can sometimes be exhausting and will regularly try your patience. As a consequence, you are quite likely to feel stress at different times during the day or the week. Often, even in anticipation of particular flashpoints, like having to get children up and dressed to get out in the morning, or during mealtimes, or in the struggle to get our children into bed, we'll feel stress.

The signs of stress are very often visible in our bodies. We can feel that our heart beats faster. We may be aware that our breathing speeds up and becomes shallower. We can often experience tightness in our muscles or cramping across our shoulders or our necks. It might be a little bit trickier to spot the way stress impacts on our thinking, but often you'll find that you don't think as clearly, or as calmly, when you are stressed. You may find that your mind is racing and that you feel agitated. It's hard to respond calmly to your children when you are experiencing these kinds of physical and cognitive symptoms.

Strangely, despite the negative impact of too much stress, it's important to feel some level of stress. If we didn't experience some stress, as a motivator, we might end up being too laid back to the point where we wouldn't bother doing anything. So a small amount of stress is helpful. Indeed, as the level of stress increases, usually our performance to achieve our particular task also increases. However, there is a point that is reached where any additional stress becomes counter-productive. Rather than motivating us to perform well, too much stress begins to negatively impact on our performance.

If children are emotionally literate and intelligent then they will be able to cope flexibly and confidently with whatever life throws their way

GETTING TO KNOW YOUR OWN STRESS LEVELS

Judging 'too much' stress is difficult. Each of us will experience stress in different ways and in different situations. For example, I know from experience that minding three children for a day is more stressful for me than giving a talk to an audience of 500 people. For you it might be the other way around. My tolerance for coping with stress may be less than yours, and so I may perceive the stress I feel to be worse than your experience of the same level of stress.

The easiest way to judge if you are getting too much stress is to pay attention to your body and your mind. The kind of physical and cognitive symptoms that I have described a little bit earlier are usually a sure sign that the stress has become too much, and that our performance is being hindered. So look out for your heart racing, your thinking getting clouded, your muscles feeling tight or clenched, your breathing feeling rushed or your mind feeling like it is racing.

If you are faced with an ongoing situation that causes you stress, you may well experience 'chronic stress'. Chronic stress can leave you feeling anxious, depressed, overwhelmed, unmotivated and angry. So whether you are feeling the effects of short-term stress (like your response to a row with your child) or long-term stress (like constantly struggling with family finances or ongoing conflict with your partner) then you need to be able to do

The easiest way to judge if you are getting too much stress is to pay attention to your body and your mind

something to manage it. If you don't manage your own stress, then you are not going to be in a position to help your children to manage their stress or even their day-to-day emotions.

I am going to give you a range of techniques that you can use to manage your stress. The one that I am going to spend most time on is the one that not only reduces stress but is also a highly effective way of managing your anger or frustration: to breathe. Breathing, or at least a particular kind of breathing called deep or abdominal breathing, is a guaranteed method of both reducing stress and giving you a momentary time-out to

Changing your breathing and your heart rate will give you a physical sensation of relaxing. On top of this, however, the process of actually counting your breaths serves as a distraction from thinking about whatever the issue was that led to you being stressed in the first place

allow you to calm down and think more clearly. If you are calm and clear thinking, then you are much more likely to react more effectively to your child's tantrum.

What deep or abdominal breathing like this is doing is slowing down the rate at which you are breathing, and this in turn slows down your heart rate. Changing your breathing and your heart rate will give you a physical sensation of relaxing. On top of this, however, the process of actually counting your breaths serves as a distraction from thinking about whatever the issue was that led to you being stressed in the first place. This effectively gives your brain a short time to switch off in 'time-out'. So, once your heart rate has slowed down and your thinking has slowed down, you are in a much stronger position to respond to whatever the issue was that led to you becoming stressed at that moment.

Breathing like this is best practised regularly at times of no stress so that you will be familiar and confident in using it whenever there are times of stress. I can almost guarantee that you will begin to respond to your child in a completely different way when you have had a moment or two out to calm down and think about what you want to achieve. This breathing technique is the most effective way of dealing with your own frustration and anger in the face of your toddler's difficult behaviour.

I like to use breathing, but there are lots of other things that you can do to generally reduce your stress and leave you in a better mood overall. Being in a better mood overall is important, because when we are in a bad mood, we tend to make bad judgements in responding to our children. When we are in a good and more relaxed frame of mind, we tend to be able to react much more effectively to whatever our children throw at us (metaphorically and literally!). So pick out the ideas and strategies from the ones below that you think will work for you.

LEARNING DEEP BREATHING

★ To practise abdominal breathing, you're best off sitting straight up in a chair with your hands resting in your lap. Then take one of your hands and place it on your abdomen just below your ribs.

★ As you breathe you are trying to create as much space as you can in your lungs by stretching out your diaphragm. Your diaphragm is the muscle at the bottom of your rib cage that sits like a blanket across your stomach and intestines. If you focus on increasing space in your lungs you will find that the air comes into your lungs naturally.

★ You are not aiming for a deep sucking motion, as if you are trying to gulp air down into your lungs. As you breathe in, therefore, you should find that the hand that is resting on your abdomen gets pushed out as your diaphragm expands and your ribs get pushed forward slightly. Your diaphragm is actually flattening out in this breathing motion and creating a vacuum in your lungs that the air will move in to fill automatically.

★ As you are breathing in, count slowly up to four, hold the air in your lungs for the count of one, and then release the air from your lungs again over the count of four. So in your head you should be having a little running commentary like 'in – 2 – 3 – 4 – hold – out – 2 – 3 – 4'.

★ That one-breath cycle should take anywhere between ten and twenty seconds depending on the speed at which you count. You then repeat the cycle three more times so that you have done four complete breaths in and out.

★ Don't do any more than four abdominal breaths at any one time because, if you do, you may find that you get dizzy. Breathing like this increases the amount of oxygen that goes into the bloodstream, and extra oxygen in the brain can lead to dizziness.

OTHER WAYS OF MANAGING YOUR STRESS

Regular relaxation is a great way of reducing stress. Sitting in front of the TV for hours at night doesn't count as relaxation. Learning a technique such as progressive muscular relaxation (PMR) or guided imagery does count. It would take too long for me to describe PMR and guided imagery here, so I won't. There are lots of CDs now that have relaxation exercises on them and guide you fully through the process – if you want to really learn to relax, then go out and buy one. Yoga is another really good way to learn to relax. Yoga induces stillness in the mind, allowing you to take a break from the racing thoughts of the day-to-day, by focusing on the body. If you don't believe me, then try it. I used to laugh at my wife when she extolled the benefits of yoga until I tried it myself. Now I practise Iyengar yoga regularly and feel better for it.

The phrase 'laughter is the best medicine' is one that is actually borne out by research. It has been shown that laughter can help you to boost your immune system functioning. What this means is that you would be less prone to getting colds and flus and, if for some reason you do get sick, you will get better that much faster. Again, because there is such a strong link between our bodies and our thoughts and our moods it's really important to keep our bodies in the best possible shape.

I used to laugh at my wife when she extolled the benefits of yoga until I tried it myself

For the same reason, taking regular exercise is also really good for reducing stress. If you can, it's great to be able to take twenty minutes of exercise that will raise your heart rate every day. That means brisk walking or jogging. It might mean swimming hard or cycling. If you live in a house with stairs, then make it your business to go up and down the stairs regularly every day even when you don't need to. If you feel yourself sweating slightly and becoming slightly out of breath during the exercise, then that's the indicator that it is having the right effect!

Along the same lines it's important to eat well. Try to reduce your caffeine and alcohol intakes. Caffeine puts extra stress on the heart and can also interfere with your sleeping, meaning that you don't get enough rest. Alcohol serves to depress your mood, and again this will muddy your thinking. The irony is, of course, that lots of us turn to alcohol or to caffeine in order to cope with stress even though they actually are counter-productive to managing stress. All those health messages that say to eat enough portions of fruit and vegetables are not to be ignored either. You need to try to make sure your own diet is well balanced, and not only will it make you feel better, but it will provide a really good role-model for your children and their eating.

Laughter can help you to boost your immune system. Taking regular exercise is also really good for reducing stress

It's also important to learn to say no as a way of dealing with stress. Sometimes we just take on too many things in the belief that we can or should be able to cope. Most of us, once we have made a commitment, will follow through on it. So the only way to avoid being in that situation is not to make the commitment in the first place. Even though at times saying no will seem selfish, you need to remember, actually, that being selfish sometimes is a good thing. If you want, you can think about selfishness as a way of you minding yourself.

GIVE YOURSELF A BREAK

Another thing that increases our stress sometimes is the high standards that we set for ourselves. We often have expectations for our own behaviour or the behaviour of others that are not actually reasonable. For example, it's not really possible to look after three children and keep a house completely spick, span and tidy (well, I can't do it anyway). It's not always possible to have your two children going in opposite directions at the same time to participate in toddler gym or swimming or horse riding or mother and baby yoga or any of the other myriad of activities that we involve our children in. So, rather than setting the bar high, set the bar at a level that you are going to achieve. If this means simplifying some things in your life, then simplify.

As a final point in managing stress, you need to hold on to the fact that you are human. If you are human, then you are going to make mistakes. It's a guaranteed part of life. Making mistakes is not a black mark against your character; rather, it's just a human trait. If you have made a mistake, whether it be in the parenting of your children, in your work life or in your relationships with your friends and family, then you need to learn from that mistake, move on and live your life. The only time that mistakes become a problem is if you keep repeating the same mistake over and over again without learning from it.

Rather than setting the bar high, set the bar at a level that you are going to achieve. If this means simplifying some things in your life, then simplify

Once you have a better handle on your stress, you will find that you can think more clearly and rationally more of the time. If you want to be able to recognize and manage your own emotions then you need to have this thinking and processing space. Let's look now at how you can understand and manage your own feelings as a precursor to managing your children's.

UNDERSTANDING AND MANAGING YOUR OWN FEELINGS

Near the start of the chapter I mentioned that we 'could' expect an adult to be able to express their feelings appropriately. I used the word 'could' advisedly. Most adults are terrible at saying what they feel. Most of the time, we act out our feelings just like a small child. An example of this might be when you have a row with your husband or partner, and he then gives you the silent treatment or walks off. Feeling upset about a project going wrong in work and coming home like an angry bear to the rest of your family is another example.

The first step to helping children understand and respond to their feelings is for us to understand our own feelings. In lots of family situations where tempers are rising or emotions are frayed the first thing we need to do is STOP. Take a few seconds out and away from the madness. Some parents like to simply count to five or ten, others like to try deep breathing like I described earlier, some will just walk away from the situation for a minute and then return. Do whatever works for you. But do something to give yourself that bit of headspace to be able to think clearly.

In lots of family situations where tempers are rising or emotions are frayed the first thing we need to do is STOP

After you have created the space, then you need to work out what you are feeling. Are you cross? Are you upset? Are you actually scared or anxious? Small children do lots of dangerous things (like jumping off walls, climbing up on counter-tops, running out into the road and so on), and our response is often to get really mad with them and give out for being so bold or impulsive. In those kinds of situations, though, it is often our terror that they were going to be harmed that leads us to being upset and subsequently getting cross.

You can imagine a mum or dad responding to their three-year-old running out on to the road in the following way:

What are you doing? You know you can't ever run into the road. How dare you run off on me like that? You are just a bold little boy, running off like that. Are you trying to get yourself killed? I can't take my eyes off you for one minute, you are so bold. Now get over here beside me. You are going nowhere, young man!

The impact of this tirade on their three-year-old son is probably to make him angry too. After all, he didn't realize that it was so dangerous to run across a road. Even if he did realize it, he probably was distracted by seeing something like a puppy on the other side and didn't think. Now he is the recipient of all this anger from his parent and he feels it is unjustified. Also, he experiences just another nail in his bold coffin, so what is the point in responding reasonably? His parent thinks he is bold no matter what.

A much better response is to recognize that we were terrified and then use that feeling to dictate our response. So breathe first and then you might say something to your child like this:

You must not run out into the road without me. I feel terrified that a car will knock you over. If an accident like that happened, it would be terrible. Running into the road is dangerous, and you may not ever do it. If you run into the road again, I will hold you by the hand for the whole walk.

In response to comments like these you can imagine a child feeling sheepish and embarrassed. They are also more likely to hear what the consequence will be for being impulsive in the future, namely that they will have to hold their parent's hand. Ultimately the main purpose of talking to your child is to get them to not run into the road in the future, so it is vital that this is the message they pick up.

DISCOVERING THE REAL MEANING OF ANGER

It is important, then, to hold on to the notion that, in order to help your child to understand and express their feelings, you have to be able to understand and express your own feelings appropriately too. This may seem obvious, but the reality is that lots of us really struggle to be aware of what we are feeling, at the time that we are feeling it. Even if we are aware of the feeling, we don't always admit to it. In the two responses above the first one shows no real awareness of the terror the parent felt, and instead that terror gets converted to anger. In the second response the parent is aware of their terror and lets the child know what that feeling is and why they have it.

Lots of us really struggle to be aware of what we are feeling, at the time that we are feeling it.

Another example of this would be that, as our own frustration rises in response to the behaviour of our toddler, the most likely response we make is to become loud and cross, giving out and demanding compliance with our rules. We rarely stop to think about whether this is the best plan or why we are even coming up with this plan. We are usually just too frustrated to think. Critically, though, we are also missing the signs in ourselves that we are cross and frustrated and that we need to stop, calm down and think about what we want to achieve with our child. This is the time to be fully aware of our annoyance and to be able to acknowledge this to ourselves and then to manage it so that it doesn't get in the way of our dealing with our child.

It sounds easy, and you are probably reading, thinking, 'I know when I am angry, of course I know when I'm angry, it's obvious to me and to everyone else.' That may be true, but if you are aware that you are angry, then why aren't you doing anything about it? If you respond angrily to your child, without filtering that anger, then you are simply acting out your anger on your child, much as they are probably acting out their anger on you.

FEELINGS COME IN MANY VARIETIES

I want you to start asking yourself the question every so often, 'What am I feeling now?' It may not seem complex but actually it can be quite difficult. I would encourage you to try to label your own feelings as descriptively as possible. There are eight main categories of feelings: anger, sadness, fear, happiness, love, disgust, shame and surprise. However, there are many different gradations of feeling within those categories. So anger could be anger, annoyance, frustration, fury and so on. Sadness could be sadness, upset, disappointment, devastation and so on. Fear could be anxiety, worry, terror and so on. Being aware of the degree of feeling and the alternative way of describing it will encourage your own emotional development and prepare you for helping your child's emotional development.

Remember that to be aware of your feelings in the heat of the moment is a tricky task. So try to avoid the heat of the moment, even if only for a few seconds, to begin the task of scanning for feelings. If you can get a handle on your feelings then you need to ask yourself, 'What will happen if I let these feelings flow?', i.e., 'If I just respond angrily will it sort out the problem?' Then you ask yourself, 'What do I need to do to sort out the problem?' In most situations the responses to these questions will be: 'If I let the feelings flow and react angrily, then it will inflame and exacerbate the situation, not solve it. In order to solve it I need to react calmly and give a clear message with both my words and my behaviour.'

Increasing your awareness of yourself and your own feelings is the first and most important step to being aware of somebody else and their feelings. Being aware of someone else and their feelings is part of empathy.

Being able to recognize the feelings of others is a skill

EMPATHY

Empathy is essentially the skill to be able to put yourself into somebody else's shoes and to try to experience the world from their perspective. In terms of feelings, this means that you can understand how somebody else might feel and respond to them in that knowledge rather than responding from the depths of your own feeling.

An example of this might be if your three-year-old son is feeling worried about going on his own to pre-school. Because of his separation anxiety he is crying every morning, refusing to get dressed, refusing to get into the car then refusing to go in the door of the pre-school. This is very wearing on a parent. It's very easy to become frustrated, not to mention stressed, about his behaviour. However, if you

Just like any other skill empathy needs to be practised again and again

use empathy, it means that you are more focused on the experience for your child of being worried, if not terrified, by the new challenge of being on their own in a pre-school. When you think of all of these behaviours as an anxiety reaction it's much easier to be tolerant and patient with your child than if you see their behaviours simply as bold or bad. If you don't see the resistant behaviour as bold or bad, then you are more likely to respond to it with understanding rather than anger.

Being able to recognize the feelings of others is a skill. Sometimes we may think that it's a natural ability; while that is probably the case, it's an ability that needs to be developed and honed. Just like any other skill it needs to be practised again and again, or else our ability to use it can become rusty.

I think we are much better at showing empathy to other adults than we are at showing it to children. When we know that someone has been bereaved, for example, we usually are very good at being able to say things to the bereaved person like 'You must really miss him,' or 'Ah, I'd say you feel so sad now.' Both of these statements, which I think most of us can manage to say, are empathy statements. Both of them identify feelings that we think the other person has. In the first one we identify a feeling of loss and in the second one we identify a feeling of sadness. Both of these statements would be experienced by the bereaved person as supportive and understanding. This kind of emotional support is absolutely crucial to children and adults alike. Sometimes we do experience feelings that we can't put a name to. It's really helpful when somebody else can put a name to them for us.

Children experience the same thing. Indeed, they have an awful lot more feelings that they probably can't put a name to, simply because they don't have the language or they haven't developed enough, emotionally, to be able to understand their feelings. This means that it becomes our job as parents to give them both a language and vocabulary for their feelings and also the ability to understand their feelings better.

The easiest way to do this is to show empathy to our children. This then allows them to understand the feelings that we think they might be having and also to associate the name for those feelings with the actual experience of those feelings.

FINDING THE RIGHT WORDS FOR THE FEELING

In psychology, one of the important things that we know is that things must be congruent. Congruence is essentially the way that things seem to match or things seem to fit. So, for example, when a child falls over and cuts their knee, it's probably quite sore. Congruence occurs when the child realizes that falling over (the experience) is associated with soreness (the feeling). So as a parent your best response is to acknowledge for your child that, yes, their knee is sore and that it does hurt. This means that the feeling they have fits with the experience that they had.

If you tell your child when they fall over, 'Stop crying, you're OK,' that doesn't fit with their experience, which is that they don't feel OK, so they end up with an incongruence between the experience (it hurts) and the feeling we are telling them (you're OK). That mismatch between the feelings we are telling them that they are having and the experience they actually are having is confusing for children and doesn't support them emotionally. In the next section I identify what I think are the most likely feelings (and reasons for those feelings) that your child might have at key flashpoints during the day.

WHAT IS YOUR CHILD FEELING?

Sometimes when you are starting off on the journey of emotionally connecting to and supporting your child, you can be a bit at sea in wondering exactly what feeling they are having. Practice and trial and error are the way forward. Even if you don't feel expert at identifying and naming feelings, it is still worthwhile. At the very least your child will appreciate the fact that you are trying to understand their emotions, and that sometimes is supportive enough. To make it a bit easier I have looked at some typical family flashpoints, or points of conflict, and tried to guess what the experience of those flashpoints might be for your child. What we will try and do is to put ourselves into the shoes of your child and to try to imagine what they are feeling and why they are feeling it. This will increase your ability to be aware of your child's feeling and to be able to empathize with it.

GETTING UP

The start of the day varies so much from child to child, from house to house and even from mood to mood. Yours may be a house where everyone leaps up in the morning full of energy and ready to face the day. Equally, you could have some real sleepy heads in the morning who never want to take themselves out of their warm beds and into the world. In the chapter on sleeping I talk a lot about ways to ensure that your child is getting enough sleep, the most important

> Even if you don't feel expert at identifying and naming feelings it is still worthwhile – your child will appreciate the fact that you are trying

of which is to ensure that they are getting to bed early enough the night before. Sometimes having more sleep can mean that your child is more alert and happier in the morning. But for the sake of this section let's assume that your child really struggles to get up when they are called.

If they have been pleasantly asleep and they get called by you, it's easy enough to imagine that they are probably going to be frustrated and cross at the disturbance. Depending on what they are due to face during the day, they could also be anxious. Any frustration is likely to be caused by not wanting to get out of a warm bed into a cold room; not having had enough sleep and therefore being grumpy; feeling persecuted by having to be called so many times; feeling indignant at the manner in which they are called; or simply not feeling ready to face the day. Anxiety could be caused by some worry about a social engagement like playing with a particular friend or going to a party. If they are in pre-school or school, it could be related to something that is happening there. These, then, would be the kinds of understanding that you would empathetically feed back to your child as you acknowledge with them that it's hard for them to get up.

EATING

Of course, eating isn't an issue for every child, and later in the book I have a whole chapter dedicated to eating and the issues involved in it. For the sake of this section, though, I am just going to focus on the feeling that your child might be having about food. Those feelings include anxiety, frustration, upset and stress. The likely reasons for those feelings are that they are afraid that they are going to get into trouble for either not eating or eating too much. They may feel constantly hassled and stressed about somebody harping on and on about what they are eating or not eating. They may feel distressed or powerless that they can't make choices about what they eat. They may be worried about the unknown

I suggest that you support your child emotionally when they are struggling with their behaviour rather than label them or give out to them

and untested flavours and textures of the food; they may feel unadventurous but forced outside of their comfort zone. They may also be feeling powerful that they can dictate to their parent how much or how little that they will eat. So, think about your child's situation regarding food, and then the chances are you might need to understand it with some of these ideas.

GETTING DRESSED AND GETTING OUT

For both getting dressed and getting out, the most usual feeling that a child has is one of frustration, and that frustration comes from being disturbed and having to do something that they don't feel ready to do. Often times, as well, they may not like the activity that you are going out to do or they may not like the people that you are going out to meet. These are the things to bear in mind when you are trying to empathize with your child's predicament.

GOING TO BED

Going to bed often produces a lot of frustration in children. Sometimes it produces anxiety also. The frustration comes from a child feeling that they are about to miss out on stuff that's going on. They may also be cross that they have been disrupted or disturbed from something that they were doing. Alternatively, they could be feeling righteously indignant at the perceived unfairness that their bedtime is earlier than somebody else's. The anxiety may be about being on their own, or they may often experience bad dreams or nightmares and so can be scared about going to sleep.

PLAYTIME

Playtimes are not always flashpoints in families but sometimes they can be. If they are, it's usually that a child is feeling angry or jealous, or perceiving that something is unjust. The reasons for these kinds of feelings are many and varied. It could be that your child is struggling to share; it could be that somebody else won't share with them; or it could be that their game has been disturbed by someone else. It could be that somebody is playing with their favourite toy. It could be that somebody is playing in their favourite place in the room; it could be that they haven't managed to build or achieve whatever it is that they are trying to do. It could be that they feel that somebody else is getting preferential treatment from you. It could be that they just want a toy that another child has. Children's playtimes are definitely times when parents need to have their full wits about them. The cause of the upset is sometimes a bit of a lottery, but it's always worth having a go at understanding it.

Of course, the feelings that I am guessing at here and the possible reasons for them are really just the starting point. You are going to know your child and you are going to be much more aware of their specific moods, preferences and relationships with others. What I am suggesting to you is that you use this knowledge to support your child emotionally when they are struggling with their behaviour, rather than label them or give out to them.

The process of understanding feelings isn't a 'softly, softly' approach. It's simply giving your child a better understanding of the totality of their experience. You are not ignoring your child's behaviour or excusing it. You simply understand it. Your child is confused sometimes because, on the one hand, they have the behaviour and the things that are happening and, on the other hand, they have the feeling. By engaging with them emotionally, you connect the feeling with the behaviour. This makes life a lot more straightforward and makes it easier to cope.

The other great thing about emotional support is that it intensifies the experience for a child of being noticed. Not only are they being attended to but they are being understood. When a child is understood it is very hard for them to continue to act out. Essentially they have no need since most acting out and tantrums are because they are frustrated and unable to express themselves in any other way. When you have understood them, then they have no more need to express themselves with the behaviour, and so, in theory, it should stop or at the very least diminish significantly.

The process of understanding feelings isn't a 'softly, softly' approach. It's simply giving your child a better understanding of the totality of their experience. You are not ignoring your child's behaviour or excusing it. You simply understand it

'DOING' EMOTIONAL SUPPORT

The best way to 'do' emotional support is to guess at the feeling that your child is having. Remember that most behaviour is preceded by some kind of feeling. All you have to do is to try to work out what it is and empathize with it. Working out what it is requires a trial-and-error approach. And, of course, like all good trial-and-error approaches, if at first you don't succeed try, try again.

Before you emotionally support your distressed child you need to spend a couple of seconds or minutes trying to get yourself calm, or at the very least becoming aware of what you are feeling yourself. As I said earlier, unless you can manage your own feelings, you are highly unlikely to help your child manage theirs.

Once you are clear-headed, you first have to try to guess what it is that your child is feeling. This is usually straightforward from the context, and hopefully the ideas I have given earlier may prompt you also. I always suggest that you use phrases like 'I wonder if you feel …', or 'You seem very …', or 'I'm guessing that you feel …', or 'It seems to me that you feel …' and so on. All of these phrases assume no certainty about the feeling. They do suggest an attempt at understanding. The difference between guessing at a feeling and being categorical about a feeling that your child has is huge.

Look at the following short conversation between a mum and her four-year-old son, John. The scenario is that John has been playing with building blocks in his room, when his mum tells him to hurry up and get ready to go out with her to the shop. She then goes off for a few minutes, and when she comes back, John is throwing his blocks around the room:

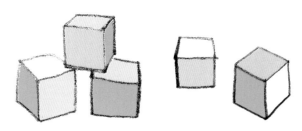

Mum: John, what are you doing? Stop flinging toys around the room. What's wrong with you?

John: Nothing.

Mum: Then stop throwing things.

John: No, I can't.

Mum: What do mean, you can't? I said stop throwing things. You're angry, you are, the bold way you are throwing things.

John: I'm not angry. *(Getting furious and starting to pull books off the shelf)*

Mum: You'd better watch out, young man. If you keep wrecking your room I'll put you out on the stairs for five minutes.

John: *(ignores his mum, and continues to throw and damage toys)*

Mum: *(getting angry herself)* Right. That's it. You can get out on those stairs right now. I have had enough of this carry-on.

John: No.

Mum: I said out on the stairs. Move it, or I'll take you out myself.

John: *(makes no move but stares provocatively at his mum)*

Mum: Enough is enough, I warned you. Come on, you. *(Grabs him by the arm and starts to drag him from the room)*

John: *(struggles and wriggles)*

Mum: Now, stay on those stairs until I tell you to get off. How dare you wreck your room and back-answer me. I'd expect it from a two-year-old, but you're four and you should know better.

Scan back through the conversation to the point at which John's mum identifies his feeling for him. She says, 'You're angry, you are, the bold way you are throwing things.' She is probably right, but the way in which she has said it is accusatory. She is telling John that he is angry (and he may not have been) and that his anger is not acceptable. All this does is to further anger John; in fact, in the example it infuriates him completely. By being definitive about his feelings she has alienated him. Rather than feeling understood and supported (the purpose of trying to identify feelings in children), he feels misunderstood and accused. So in this example the mum has missed out on the opportunity to understand things from John's perspective. Even though she recognizes that he is angry she isn't able to let John know that she understands why he might be angry. So, to go back to the example, the mum has John at the stairs. Let's see how the rest of the scene plays out.

Mum: *(realizing that she now has John on the stairs but actually needs him in the car to get to the shops)* **Even though you are so bold I'm not going to leave you on the stairs, but by God you deserve to be. So stop sitting there and take that sullen look off your face. Put on your shoes; we are going out. I still have to get to the shops, and they are going to be closing soon. I need the patience of Job with you.**

John: *(realizing that he is still going to be taken shopping gets more frustrated and starts crying loudly)*

Mum: **What is your problem? Can you not do anything I ask? You are such a spoilt little brat sometimes. Look, I am stopping your punishment. I said you don't have to keep sitting on the stairs. You'd think you'd be happy about that. Will you get your shoes on and get into that car? If you don't get into the car right away I am warning you …**

John: *(realizing that his playtime and game are disrupted one way or the other, continues to bawl and continues to be uncooperative)*

Mum:	I don't understand you. It is like you deliberately try to wreck my head. Will you please stop crying? Stop it, or I'll give you something to cry over.
John:	*(doesn't stop because he can't at this stage – he has wound himself up into a state of near hysteria)*
Mum:	*(slaps him hard across the leg)* **There, you asked for that. Now get into that car and stop screaming. Stop it. Stop it ...** *(She roughly puts on his shoes and half drags, half carries him to the car. Shopping is hell)*

It is no surprise that shopping is hell because by that point all is lost for John and his mum. His mum feels furious but helpless. She probably sees his behaviour as atrocious and wonders how anyone could put up with that. Unfortunately, she is also feeling completely powerless and probably ineffective too. She has tried punishing him to get him to behave, and in each case it just made the situation worse. From her point of view the 'management techniques' that she believes she is using are ineffective. She ends up having to bring this uncooperative 'demon' to the shops, simply because she must, and I would guess that, once she is in the shops, she buys him off with a treat just to get him to stop crying and embarrassing her.

Most behaviour is preceded by some kind of feeling. All you have to do is to try to work out what it is and empathize with it

From John's perspective the moment is probably lost when his mum fails to understand why he is throwing his toys. From that point on his mum displays less and less understanding and becomes harsher and harsher in her treatment of him. I'd be willing to guess that both John and his mum know where the scenario is headed right from the start, and neither of them can think of a way to head it in a new or different direction. John and his mum are stuck in a really negative spiral of interaction. One action leads inevitably to another. Even though it is negative, I'd say that John at least feels noticed by his mum, even if he doesn't feel understood. His mum, while not feeling very effective, at least probably feels she is in charge and has shown John who is the boss. This means that they are getting enough from the interaction to make it likely to happen again. Unfortunately, it comes at the cost of both of them feeling angry and disconnected from each other.

I want you now to start the scenario again, in your head. Mum wants John to finish playing so that she can take him off with her to the shops.

Mum: John, we'll be going to the shops in five minutes. That means you have to finish up playing and put on your shoes and coat. I'll be back in a minute to help you.

John: *(not wanting to be disturbed in his game, feels cross and ignores his mum's request. When he hears her coming back after the minute he starts throwing his blocks)*

Mum: Hey, what's going on? You are throwing your blocks around the room. You are messing up your own game.

John: I don't care.

Mum: If you are throwing your blocks and wrecking your building I am guessing you are feeling cross about something.

John: *(ignores his mum but stops throwing stuff)*

Mum: I wonder if you weren't ready to stop your building game when I told you that you had to get ready to come to the shops with me. It's never nice to be disturbed.

John: I hate it. I don't want to go to the shops.

Mum: You say that you hate being disturbed and you don't want to come to the shops. That must make it hard for you when you have to come, then, even if you don't want to. Unfortunately, we must go to the shops or we will have no milk for breakfast.

John: I don't care.

Mum: Oh, you do seem very cross and put out about having to come with me. It is hard being disturbed. I never like being disturbed either. Unfortunately you have to come because I can't leave you behind; you are too small, and it might be scary for you. When we come back from the shops, though, I'll have time to help you build some more. *(She holds his hand as she leads him down to the hallway to get his coat and shoes)*

John: *(still feeling grumpy, but offering no resistance as he realizes that his game is disturbed anyway and that his mum understands that this is annoying for him)* When we get home I want you to play for ages.

Mum: We'll see when we get home. I will have some time to play but I will also have other jobs to do, so we'll make sure we share the time fairly. I like building things with you. Will we walk or drive to the shop?

John: Let's drive.

Mum: Ah, you want to get back as quickly as possible. OK then. Let's go.

The outcome of this conversation is much happier for both John and his mum. John still has to stop playing and his mum never moves the goalposts about having to come to the shops. What is different is that, when his mum recognizes how he is feeling (based on the toys being fired around the room – often a giveaway!), she checks it with him rather than tells him. She also tries to guess at the source of his frustration and crossness. Even though John didn't verbally acknowledge either of these guesses, his behaviour responds to the understanding. Initially, he stops throwing things and then he lets himself be led from the room. By the end of the chat his mum has distracted him into deciding on the mode of transport, and John is, at this point, engaged in the shopping trip.

It is possible that John could have kept up the crossness all the while he was being led to the hallway and he could have resisted. If that had been the case, I would have encouraged the mum to bring him, unwillingly, but still empathizing with how much of a struggle he was finding it being disturbed. The unfortunate reality for John is that he was always going to be disturbed anyway and he is never going to enjoy the disruption. As his parent you just have to accept that and understand it rather than trying to deny, counteract or prevent it. You still need to be powerful and authoritative in ensuring he comes with you but you do it by understanding him and showing him in your words that you understand. So, by feeding into his upset and encouraging it by bringing it out into the open, you allow him to get over it rather than continue to be faced with it.

If you recall, the research on emotional intelligence shows that, when you deliberately engage with your child's feelings, it sets them up on a path to be able to cope with many of life's challenges.

These are the steps of 'doing' emotional support that John's mother followed.

⭐ To become aware of your child's emotion or feeling (noticing the angry throwing of the blocks in the first instance)

⭐ To recognize that this feeling is an opportunity for intimacy and learning (deliberately making the time to talk rather than simply giving out and bustling him out the door)

⭐ To listen empathetically to your child and to acknowledge their feelings (her statement 'If you are throwing your blocks and wrecking your building I am guessing you are feeling cross about something', and later when she responds, 'You say that you hate being disturbed and you don't want to come to the shops. That must make it hard for you when you have to come, then, even if you don't want to')

⭐ To help your child find words to label the feeling that they are having (like when his mum says, 'I am guessing you are feeling cross about something')

⭐ To continue to set limits while exploring strategies to solve the problem at hand (this can be seen when the mum stays firm about going: 'Unfortunately you have to come because I can't leave you behind, you are too small, and it might be scary for you.

When we come back from the shops, though, I'll have time to help you build some more')

At home I try to engage emotionally with my children all the time. It doesn't stop them having tantrums or getting upset but it does radically speed up their recovery from the tantrum and their re-entry to the family plan or activity. It also doesn't prevent me from having to dress them sometimes against their will, or insist that they wear a coat or hat, or ensure that they brush their teeth. It just shows them that, when there are unpalatable things to be done, it can be upsetting and frustrating, and, despite the upset or frustration, they still have to do the thing. But at least they know, too, that someone understands the frustration they feel. Being understood is always comforting.

KEY POINTS TO REMEMBER

> Emotional intelligence can be developed and has five main components: knowing your emotions; managing your emotions; motivating yourself; recognizing feelings in others; and managing relationships.

> Emotionally intelligent children are more resilient and better able to cope with whatever life throws their way.

> Understanding and dealing with your own stress is a precursor to trying to understand and manage your feelings.

> Some stress is necessary in life, but too much stress is counter-productive and actually gets in the way.

> We feel stress in our bodies, our minds and our moods, and so in managing the stress we need to address relaxing ourselves physically and becoming more positive in our thinking and not over-extending ourselves.

- Understanding our own feelings requires us to stop and think about what is going on.

- There are eight main categories of feelings: anger, sadness, fear, happiness, love, disgust, shame and surprise.

- If you don't recognize and manage your own feelings you will act them out on your child and make the situation worse.

- Emotionally supporting children requires empathy.

- Empathy is our ability to put ourselves in their shoes and understand how they might feel from their perspective.

- Children who feel emotionally understood do not have the same need to show their distress, upset or anger by acting it out with bad behaviour.

- There is a range of feelings that you can expect children to feel at typical flashpoints in a family's day.

- Doing emotional support means labelling and understanding the emotions our children have to help them to understand and learn a language for what they are feeling.

4

COPING WITH TANTRUMS

HOLDING ON TO SANITY WHEN ALL AROUND YOU ARE LOSING THEIRS

Toddler meltdown is never pleasant to witness and even less fun to have to deal with. The fear of going to the supermarket with a toddler in tow, which could be known as 'tantrumophobia' (even though the dictionary might not back me up!), sets the hearts and shopping speeds of many parents racing. It is amazing how quickly you can get around a supermarket if you have to. For those with toddlers it is usually the time taken to eat one small bread roll and a bar of chocolate or a bag of crisps.

The reality is, though, that we can't always help our children to avoid those tantrums. What we rarely pay heed to is that children's tantrums are another form of communication. We usually don't see it that way and instead often rush into conflict with our sons and daughters at the first sign of their anger brewing. Most tantrums occur because your child has no more effective way to express their anger and frustration. When we then respond to their anger with our own anger you may wonder whether we have any better expressive skills ourselves!

I remember an evening in our house when everything just seemed to be slipping away from me. My wife was out for the evening and had taken the baby with her. I was left behind with our two older children for what should have been a straightforward evening of playtime, bedtime routine and then time for me when all were asleep. It started to go wrong after dinner as I was reading through the post that had arrived and realized that I had missed the deadline for an application that I had submitted. Then, my two children, aged six and four at the time, decided to fight over whose train engine should lead the way on the track.

Children's tantrums are a form of communication, and most occur because our child has no more effective way to express their anger and frustration

Rather than get involved and help them to negotiate a settlement I let them fight it out until their screams became piercing. Then, already feeling annoyed about missing my deadline, I decided that I had had enough and roared, helpfully, from the kitchen that they had better be quiet or I would give them a reason to scream. Unsurprisingly, they didn't need another reason to scream and they certainly weren't bothered by my lacklustre intervention, and their disagreement deepened. Tired and frustrated, I stormed into the sitting room, grabbed the train engines and started to pack up the train set. I hadn't thought that the screams could get louder, but they did. You will have spotted, of course, that I had missed a few golden rules of managing children's behaviour, but I like to think that I am just human.

Anyway, my four-year-old daughter went off 'sulking' at the sudden and unforeseen (not to mention un-forewarned) ending of the game. My six-year-old son decided to have a go at me for being so unfair and for not telling them that I would end the game and for shouting at them and for being mean in general. He managed to express all of this while he screamed and hammered on the floor with one of the remaining train-track pieces. He may have had a point, but I wasn't in the mood to hear it.

What ensued was ugly, and in retrospect I wasn't proud of it. I shouted back at him and, because I was twenty-seven years older, I won the argument by sheer force of my will and because I could lift him up and carry him to his bed, half an hour earlier than he should have been going. Again, I was breaking all of my own rules about not using bed as a place of punishment and not using time-out as a punishment. Sometimes, though, when it is bad, it is just very bad.

Eventually, I calmed down. I went back to my son and daughter and apologized for my behaviour, as it had been totally out of order. With my new-found composure I was able to empathize with their plight both in disagreeing about the train engines and in my son's accurate complaints about my handling of the situation. I was struck by how much greater an impact my mishandling of the situation had had than the original disagreement and the start of their tantrum with each other. The perceived injustice and rejection of my actions had left my son distraught and my daughter frightened. We patched things up and regained our equilibrium.

> We can't always help our children to avoid tantrums but you – and I – have a responsibility to our children to remain adults and help them to learn how to cope with their tantrums

What the anecdote illustrates to me (and why I remember it so clearly even though it happened a couple of years ago) is that my reaction was so powerful and inflammatory that it had the potential to devastate my relationship with my children. My tantrum was far more dangerous than theirs. You – and I – have a responsibility to our children to remain adults and help our children to learn how to cope with their tantrums.

THE FUNCTION AND PURPOSE OF TANTRUMS

When I talk about tantrums I am thinking about a child losing the plot entirely and screaming, wailing, crying, maybe stamping feet, or slamming doors or lying on the ground. I am not talking or thinking about a child whingeing, moaning or simply giving out about their lot in life. The ideas I have, though, will work with the latter group of behaviours, but I am mostly focused on situations where children can barely think straight because they have managed to get themselves so upset.

> It is hard to accept that your child's tantrum may have a purpose, or a function, other than to simply annoy you and drive you up the wall

It is hard to accept that your child's tantrum may have a purpose, or a function, other than to simply annoy you and drive you up the wall. After all, their melt-down is sometimes completely unprovoked and at times patently unwarranted.

Most tantrums, however, can be classified as resulting from one of two things: a need to express frustration or a need to get noticed.

The world can be a very frustrating place for a toddler and pre-schooler. Lots of things happen that they have no control over; lots of things happen that they don't intend; and lots of things happen that they can't resolve. On top of that, most toddlers can't even express their frustrations in words because their language skills are not well enough developed. This is a tricky old spot to be in. Toddlers, of course, try to get out of it by having tantrums.

When the world frustrates you because you can't have any ice-cream and you want ice-cream, you need to let the world know. When your language skills are not well enough developed to explain to your mother or father that, actually, not having this ice-cream will be devastating for you, you don't have too many options. In this instant your whole life centres on having this one desire met, and you have to let people around you understand this. If you could, you'd explain to them that you'd be happy to swap any other thing they have ever given you for this ice-cream right now. If you could, you'd explain to them

Showing upset through shouting, screaming and banging seems to work every time for small children

that not having the ice-cream will actually cause a deep pain that they probably don't understand but need to take your word for. However, all of these factors are caught up in your frustration, and your language skills are letting you down because it is just too difficult to say all this. Arise and enter the tantrum.

Showing upset through shouting, screaming and banging seems to work every time for small children. I think that we all could translate the tantrum to the feelings and desires that I attributed to this particular toddler who isn't getting the ice-cream; we just don't. This is the nub of the problem; because if most parents do understand that their child is frustrated and acting out because of it, they don't usually show it. Most of us, most of the time, respond angrily to our child's tantrum, no matter what the reason for it. Even though we recognize that they are probably just frustrated, we still get cross at the manner in which they choose to show us that frustration.

WHY TANTRUMS WORK

What I think happens then, and why tantrums work for children, is that, when we respond, albeit angrily, to the tantrum, our child feels acknowledged – we have recognized that something is wrong even if we haven't recognized what it is! So even though we haven't shown that we understand their frustration we have shown that we notice their frustration. This means that tantrums as a way of expressing frustration become effective, too, as a way of getting a response from adults.

Not only do parents notice by getting angry, they often respond, after the tantrum reaches a particular intensity, by giving in and getting the ice-cream as a way of getting the tantrum stopped. This is a fatal error! At this point your child has realized that their tantrum has not only expressed their frustration effectively but it has also succeeded in resolving the source of their frustration. They have learned, too, that their frustration is most likely to be relieved at the point of greatest intensity of their tantrum. In the future, unsurprisingly, they will head straight for maximum-strength tantrum to get what they want and remove the frustration.

Children will be frustrated, just like we get frustrated, and in life we can't always take away the source of that frustration. So rather than simply removing the source of frustration, and in the process justifying for your child that the tantrum was worth it, we need to let our children be frustrated and instead teach them better ways of coping with the frustration other than tantrums. This, of course, ties back into my belief that we need to teach our children the language of feelings if we want them to be able to express those feelings more appropriately.

LOOKING FOR ATTENTION – ANY ATTENTION WILL DO

Before getting stuck into how to respond to tantrums, though, let's quickly look at the other most common function of a tantrum – attention-seeking. Children will use tantrums as a tool for getting noticed. Even small children quickly realize that the bigger their upset and tantrum, the greater the response of their parents. Children are not really very discriminating when it comes to attention-seeking. Most small children don't mind whether they are being praised or being given out to as long as they have the whole and undivided attention of their parent during that time. As a result tantrums are a great way of getting and holding that 100 per cent attention. As I mentioned earlier, simply being acknowledged is enough for most children and reinforces their belief that, if I'm not happy about something, I need to scream and shout and kick my feet, and people will notice.

You can usually tell by the context whether a tantrum is about frustration or attention. If your child is denied something they want, if they can't achieve something they believe they should be achieving, or if they lose something precious, then the chances are that frustration is behind it all. Depending on our response, though, our children will learn that, actually, a tantrum is a good way to get noticed and so they may choose to have a tantrum just for attention. So, if there is no obvious source of frustration and you are aware that your child may have been missing out on your time, then their tantrum can probably be translated as a desire to be noticed by you.

Most small children don't mind whether they are being praised or being given out to as long as they have the whole and undivided attention of their parent during that time

BLOW-UPS AND MELT-DOWNS

I am always struck by the imagery of these two terms that we commonly use to describe tantrums. The first, blow-up, seems to characterize a dramatic disintegration of the child with an accompanying danger for anyone around who gets caught in the blast. It suggests a fiery, almost aggressive tantrum that is hazardous to come close to. Melt-down, on the other hand, while also suggestive of disintegration, seems to be more like the internal breaking-down of the child's coping strategies. It is as if everything merges into one for the child, and they lose the capacity to think separately and clearly. Both the images make sense for different children and sometimes even for one child. You can imagine how sometimes your own child is in a frustrated heap of a tantrum on one occasion and at other times is like a writhing and twitching live wire that is sparking and cracking off anything it comes into contact with.

Of course, all of these images really remind us that it is worth trying to avoid that situation in the first place. Distraction and diversion are the tools to use.

You can imagine how sometimes your own child is in a frustrated heap of a tantrum on one occasion and at other times is like a writhing and twitching live wire that is sparking and cracking off anything it comes into contact with

DISTRACTING AND DIVERTING TO AVOID TANTRUMS

Sometimes it is just not worth meeting a tantrum head-on. Most of us begin to recognize the patterns of our children from early on. We recognize their sleep habits, we become aware of their eating habits and we start to notice patterns to their behaviour. Children's predictability is a bit of a bonus when it comes to behaviour. Their predictability means that we can get some advance warning of when they are about to 'blow up' or 'melt down'. If we have warning then sometimes we can sidestep the issue and help them to avoid the tantrum in the first place. I would imagine that you already naturally use distraction with your children to keep the peace or to get them to do something that you know they would not normally do.

I was trying to teach my five-year-old daughter to ride her bike without stabilizers. We were on the grass, so that, if she fell over, it wouldn't hurt too much. Our garden has a slight slope down to a brambly hedge at the back. My daughter has a passion for picking blackberries (like most children I have known), and so I kept telling her to look at the brambles to see if she could see any blackberries growing. The purpose of this was twofold. I wanted her to take her attention away from the fact that my hand wasn't holding on to the back of the saddle after she got going and I wanted her to look forward and into the distance to help her balance rather than looking down at her hands or the pedals. Despite my best attempts at distraction in this fashion my daughter steadfastly refused to be drawn away from her hyper-vigilance of the bike and its movement. Needless to say she kept falling off, and I ended up frustrated that she hadn't got the hang of her balance. My daughter also got frustrated and decided that she didn't want to learn to ride without stabilizers anyway.

I then got really worried and started thinking that my daughter 'should' be able to cycle her bike at this stage. I kept encouraging her to get back out and continue trying to cycle, but she dug her heels in at that point and decided (I think) that the more pressure I put on her the less she was going to cooperate. For days in a row I kept hassling her to

Distraction and diversion are the tools to use

go out and try again. In true dad fashion I had forgotten that her knowing how to cycle was her issue and not mine. Thankfully, I have a wife with much more sense and reason, who told me to back off. Once I got over my affront at being told how to behave, I did back off. Three months later, my daughter decided, one day, that she wanted to cycle and asked me to help her to get on her bike, as it was a bit wobbly, and to hold it steady as she got ready to push off. She then pushed off and cycled, without her stabilizers and without her dad.

The point of this story is that distraction (looking ahead for blackberries) is a good idea, and in theory it should work, but it doesn't always. In addition, though, the story illustrates that sometimes our expectations of our children exceed their own. We have desires and hopes for what they are ready to achieve and so we can easily push them forward when they are not ready. If that happens, it can lead to a withdrawal from them, and we need to heed the message to pull back also. Children grow and develop in their own time, and when the time is right for them they will take their steps forward.

> **The point of this story is that distraction (looking ahead for blackberries) is a good idea, and in theory it should work, but it doesn't always**

In order to use distraction and diversion effectively with tantrums, the first step is to try to be aware of the pattern that your child follows when they are about to slip into tantrum mode. What are the early-warning signs that a tantrum is likely to ensue? For example, you may know that every time you have to say 'no' to your child it will result in a tantrum. You may notice that, just before a tantrum starts, your child will try a bout of whingeing. You may notice that, just before a tantrum, their hands form into little fists, or their breathing gets noticeably shallower and faster.

You need to use the early-warning signs that your child gives to know when to distract. Once your child is in full flight it is almost impossible to distract them, and in fact it is usually impossible to get any reason from them at all, even by talking to them.

HEADING OFF THE STORM

If you notice a tantrum brewing, you might try these distractions:

☆ Change the conversation, especially by sounding surprised or like you have just remembered something

☆ Comment that they look like they are going to get mad and then move in and initiate some rough-and-tumble horseplay

☆ Comment that there is a lot of energy growing in the room and suggest using it to have horse races outside, or decide to have an impromptu disco or a skipping marathon

☆ Suddenly pretend to be an angry tiger roaring and invite everyone else to do the same

☆ Remind everyone of the next nice thing due to happen and get them moving to prepare for it. This might be something as simple as it being nearly suppertime or it may be that you are going out on trip somewhere

☆ Use any natural distraction such as someone coming to the door or notice a bird at the window or the action of a pet

☆ Spot a favourite toy and start playing with it, encouraging your child to show you what to do.

As soon as you start thinking about distractions you will find that lots more come to mind. Essentially they fall into the categories of either channelling the energy or helping your child to forget about the source of frustration. If the source of frustration cannot be ignored, because it has to happen, then the channelling distractions often work best. Your child may be feeling a lot less oppositional after you have been rolling on the floor or bed with them. You'll remember from the discussion in the chapter on play that you can actually characterize the anger/frustration in the horseplay, and so it can often get expressed or worked out more easily.

If distraction doesn't do it, or you miss the window when it is likely to be effective, then you'll have to deal with the tantrum. Let's look now at what you need to do.

RESPONDING TO TANTRUMS

You'll have a few things to remember when it comes to responding to and dealing with tantrums. You will be trying to work out what is behind the tantrum, you will be trying to remember to keep your own feelings in check and you will be trying to decide on the best strategy for dealing with it.

Hopefully, the context will clearly tell you whether the tantrum is due to frustration or attention-seeking. Hopefully, you will also have practised the deep-breathing exercises that I spoke about in the chapter on feelings. So I am going to assume that you are approaching the tantrum armed with knowledge and calm.

Let's look initially at frustration-based tantrums. The key to responding to these kinds of tantrums is to ensure that you give your child a message that you understand their frustration but that while they are having the tantrum you can do nothing to help to sort it out. As soon as they are calm, then you can help. Let's take an example of where a four-year-old daughter, Chloe, has 'lost' a favourite doll. Her mum knows that the doll is probably not lost per se, it is just most likely to be buried in the jumble of toys that she stuffs into the wardrobe. Chloe comes to her mum, already crying about the missing doll, feeling the pain of both the loss and the frustration of not being able to find her.

Chloe: I can't find my dolly. She's lost. *(cries even harder for effect)*

Mum: Which dolly? 'Sarah'?

Chloe: Yeah, I can't find her. She's lost.

Mum: I doubt she's lost. She's probably just gone missing amongst all your other toys. Did you look in your wardrobe?

Chloe: Yeah and she's not there. *(Starts to lose control of her crying)*

Mum: Take it easy, Chloe, why don't you play with your horse set, and we'll look

	later for Sarah? *(Trying to distract)*
Chloe:	*(now wailing)* **I just want Sarah.**
Mum:	**There, there.** *(Comfortingly putting an arm around Chloe and hugging her)* **I know it is hard when dolls go missing. You seem very upset. Oh, you poor thing, losing a toy is upsetting. It'll be OK.**
Chloe:	*(not sure if it is OK to stop crying yet and so continues)*
Mum:	*(staying calm by breathing deeply and using a very gentle tone of voice)* **I can guess you are really upset. But when you are crying and screaming like that I can't help you. When you calm down, we can try to sort it out and find Sarah.**
Chloe:	*(persists in crying and drops to the floor)*
Mum:	*(maintains her calm, gentle and warm tone)* **I can hear and see you're upset. You are now sitting on the floor. It would be really sad to think that she is lost and probably really frustrating that you can't play with her right now when you want to. When you keep crying I can't help you. But, as soon as you are calm, I can help you. You can stay sitting on the floor and when you are ready to be calm and have stopped crying we'll talk some more.**

At that point the mum turns away and resumes whatever task she was doing. What she has managed to achieve is to let Chloe know that she understands how she is feeling. All of her words, her body language and her tone of voice reinforce this empathy. The mum has also managed to be clear and quite firmly consistent that she is not going to pay her any more attention until she is dealing better with those feelings and able to be calmer in sorting out the problem. The mum then listens carefully for the first sign that Chloe is stopping her crying. This is usually when some air seems to get into the lungs and the crying turns to occasional sobs and sniffs. That is the point at which the mum needs to turn back to Chloe and comment on how she seems to have stopped crying and is obviously feeling calmer and ready for some help to find the doll. If Chloe does indeed hold on to her feelings, then the mum needs to follow through on what she offered and go and help to look for the doll.

If you remember, children who are frustrated or upset are most likely to be having a tantrum as their way of expressing

> Your task, then, is to understand and empathize with the frustration and upset but not give so much attention that your child begins to learn that a tantrum not only gets them understanding but it also gets them unlimited attention

it. Your task, then, is to understand and empathize with the frustration and upset but not give so much attention that your child begins to learn that a tantrum not only gets them understanding but it also gets them unlimited attention. So, after spending some time showing your child you can understand their plight, you then leave them to get on with the tantrum and you deliberately ignore them and the tantrum until it is over. This may mean that you give the same simple message 'When you are calm we can sort this out' on a few different occasions, particularly if your child is persistent and tenacious in shoving their tantrum into your face.

Most children who have been understood and empathized with in this way will get over their tantrum quite quickly. Be alert for signs of their calmness as you need to be ready then to respond to them when they act more calmly, just like you said you would.

You'll notice, too, that, while I do recommend that you intentionally ignore the tantrum at a point, I don't recommend sending your child to time-out. I'd be afraid that your child would get the wrong message if you sent them away and I'll explain all the reasons why further on in the section on time-outs.

MANAGING THE ATTENTION-SEEKING SPECIAL-ISSUE TANTRUM

Now I want to go through a strategy with you for dealing with attention-seeking tantrums. Not that the strategy is radically different, but there are a few important differences to the strategy described above.

When your child is deliberately winding themselves up into a tantrum just to get your attention, it is important that they don't get lots of that attention. Most children have a few gala performances stored up for when they just have to get noticed. Typically in lots of families, you can get these attention-seeking tantrums just after you have been away. So when you are coming in from work, everyone wants a piece of you, and sometimes your toddler will seek their share by having an almighty melt-down.

I recall the first time I and my wife went away for an overnight without our two eldest children. Their little brother had been born and was still breast-feeding, so he came with us when we went down to Kerry for a funeral. Our older two were aged six and four at the time. We kept in regular contact, and everything was going great back home as their granny and grandad were down to mind them. When we got back the next evening, there was a honeymoon period of about seven minutes when everyone was just delighted to see everyone and stories about the activities in our absence were being excitedly told. Then, almost as if on cue, both of the older children lost the plot and started fighting with each other and with us. My parents naturally tried to reassure us that all had been great while we were gone.

> When your child is deliberately winding themselves up into a tantrum just to get your attention, it is important that they don't get lots of that attention

I'm sure it had been. Thankfully, we recognized that their tantrums were probably a reaction to having missed us while we were gone and then looking for us to notice them now that we were back.

As an aside, children find it very stressful, at times, to be separated from their parents. Often they will keep a lid on that stress while you are gone. After all, they have to be able to cope minute by minute and hour by hour while you are not there. If they let their stress overwhelm them, as it may threaten to do, then they wouldn't cope and instinctively they know this. So they use a really common psychological defence – denial – for the period that you are away. They deny to themselves that the stress is there or that it is impacting on them. Once you return, though, there is no more need for them to keep denying the feelings of stress, and so they can let their defences down and then they are simply reacting and responding to their stress. Surprise, surprise, that response is to have a tantrum or get really upset or to start fighting.

Of course, you don't have to go away and return in order for children to have a tantrum to get your attention. When children learn that having a tantrum gets them lots of attention, it is not surprising that they then turn to tantrums whenever they want notice. In a busy household it is not uncommon for parents to be occupied with tasks and chores while their children amuse themselves. What often then happens is that they actually do only notice their child when something goes wrong or a tantrum occurs.

As a precursor to, and balancing of, dealing with attention-seeking tantrums you need also to make sure that you are spending enough time catching your child being good. This means that your child will learn that they can get notice for things other than tantrums. Unless your child knows that they can get your attention in other, more positive, ways, it will be almost impossible to prevent attention-seeking tantrums.

> **As a precursor to, and balancing of, dealing with attention-seeking tantrums you need also to make sure that you are spending enough time catching your child being good**

Let's assume, therefore, that you are doing the whole play thing with your child, and they do indeed get noticed for acting in good ways as well as for acting in bold ways. When you are then faced with a tantrum that is purely seeking your attention, you need to respond firmly and consistently. The message that you want to give your child is that 'I recognize you are upset, but having a tantrum is not the way to get my attention. Only when you can be calm will you get my attention.'

Like the earlier strategy for coping with frustration tantrums, you need to give this message both verbally and through your actions. With attention-seeking, though, your recognition of their feeling is based on their need to get noticed rather than frustration. To help your child recognize this you would say things like: 'You seem very upset and I think you are being so upset in order to get me to notice you,' or you might want to say, 'When you keep screaming I think you want me to realize that you want me to spend time with you.' As with the earlier approach you have initially helped your child to recognize what is really going on. You then need to give your child the key message that actually the tantrum won't get your attention but calmness will.

So you then say to your child, 'Being cross won't get me to spend more time with you, but when you are calm, I will spend time with you,' or as an alternative you may say, 'When you are calm, I will be able to talk to you, but when you are acting angrily, I will not talk to you.' You can then give them some space to have time-out (according to my guide to time-out) and just as before you then deliberately ignore your child until you see the first signs of them being calmer. You do need to be vigilant and catch that calming moment. As soon as you have evidence that they are being calmer, you step in and say, 'You seem calmer. It is much easier to talk to you now. I like to spend time with you when you are calm …' and then continue into a warm and engaged conversation.

Deliberately ignoring your child is a tricky business

Deliberately ignoring your child is a tricky business. You don't want to reject them and you don't send them away. You just want to avoid giving them undue attention for having a tantrum. You are not trying to punish your child with the ignoring, you are just trying to let them know that screaming angrily is not the way to get your notice. It is really important, therefore, that, before you withdraw your attention, you let your child know that you will be doing this and the reason why. Keeping your tone of voice calm and warm is central to this. If you stay warm and understanding but firm and decisive you will not be dismissing them and their feelings; instead, you will be supporting them. If you find that you are sounding angry and cold, then the chances are that, no matter what you say, they will be feeling rejected, and the tantrum may very well continue.

BE WARY OF USING TIME-OUT AS PUNISHMENT

Unfortunately, time-out has been promoted recently as the panacea to pretty much every behavioural problem that a child presents you with. I have heard other professionals suggest time-out for attention-seeking behaviour, time-out for tantrums, time-out for hitting, time-out for not responding to your requests/demands, time-out for being bold, and the list seems almost endless. In all those situations the time-out is being put forward as a punishment or consequence for some misbehaviour on the child's part.

In my opinion, this is an incorrect use of time-out. I don't believe that time-out should be a consequence or punishment. Time-out has a place in managing children's behaviour but only as an opportunity to give you or your child time to cool off and calm down. I believe that using time-out as a punishment is the emotional equivalent of slapping. When you punish a child by sending them off to 'the step' or to their room or to a 'bold chair', you are effectively giving them a message that their behaviour, and by inference they themselves, are so abhorrent to you that you can't even bear to have them in the room. The message underlying your punishment time-out is: 'You are so bold you have to go away now and stay away until I am ready to have you back.' These messages are hugely rejecting of children. When children feel rejected, you are more likely to see an increase in difficult behaviour than a reduction. Alternatively, by rejecting them, you may distance yourself from your child such that, at important times in the future, they may not feel able to confide in you.

Time-out as a punishment is usually resorted to when parents are at their wit's end and can no longer cope with or manage their children's behaviour. Using it to punish when you and they are inevitably angry and cross also can tell your child, 'When you or the other people are cross and angry, you should reject them.' If a child learns this message, then in the longer

> **Time-out has a place in managing children's behaviour but only as an opportunity to give you or your child time to cool off and calm down**

term it will impact on their style of relating to others. When they get angry, they too may push people away, believing that to emotionally engage is wrong. They will possibly be learning from you a core belief that, when you get angry with someone, you separate yourself from them. Imagine every time you have a fight with your partner that they pull away or try to push you away – it makes resolving the difficulties very hard.

A NEW APPROACH TO TIME-OUT

Time-out, when used to give time and space to calm down, is a very different tool altogether. I have suggested at several points along the way in this book that parents need to take time for themselves to breathe, count to five or ten, or at times walk away in order to calm themselves down enough to be able to effectively manage the situation they find themselves in with their child. This is essentially time-out, but it is the parents taking time-out. Those few seconds may be enough time for a parent to feel less angry and become more focused on the outcome that they want to achieve. The principle with a child is exactly the same.

You want them to have time to breathe, calm down and think more clearly. So that is what you tell them. Your time-out regime is about creating space, ensuring that the misbehaviour stops and giving opportunities for normal life to continue. If we take an example of a boy hitting his little baby sister, then a typical verbal message to go along with time-out might be: 'You may not hit your sister. Hitting is not allowed in our family. If you hit, then you must sit over here (indicate some chair or sofa or bed in the room you are in that is away from their sister) and, when you can play calmly, then you can join back in.' As you are indicating the place to sit, you physically guide or carry them to that place. When you have finished your message about them rejoining the play when they are calm, you then reduce your attention to them. This is not the time for lecturing about the rights and wrongs of hitting or inter-sibling rivalry! Those conversations can happen later when the situation is calmer and the hitting has stopped.

If the problem is a three-year-old tantrum, then you may be saying something like: 'You seem really upset. (Starting off with empathy is always a bonus!) When you are so upset I can't understand you and can't help you. Take a break over here (indicate somewhere comfy to sit in the room with you) and, when you are calm, we can try to sort it out. Until you are calm, I can't help you.' In both these examples you may continue to be in the room but busy yourself doing something else that doesn't give direct attention to your child. If they are trying to calm down and trying to explain something to you in a calmer way, then it is OK to respond.

This notion of actually being with your child if they are misbehaving and sticking with them and their difficult feelings is critical to the success of using time-out in the way I am suggesting. The underlying message you are giving your child by sticking with them is: 'You are important, and that is why I am still here with you, but your behaviour is not OK, and you need to stop it and be calm so that we can move on from here.'

The length of time in punishment time-out is often given as a minute per year of the child's age and one extra minute. This strikes me as madness. I have witnessed the scenes of parents struggling with their five-year-old to keep them sitting on the bottom step of the stairs, nominally for six minutes. The initial issue that led to the time-out being enforced has long been forgotten, and instead the situation has morphed into a battle of wills to see who has the greater power in the relationship. The battle occurs because the parent must keep the child in time-out for the full six minutes or they lose face in front of their child, and their child will rightly learn that the parent doesn't mean what they say. The child, meanwhile, is cross about having to be taken from the room and is going to do their level best to show the parent that they can't rule their life. For both sides the stakes are high, and neither is going to want to give in first. So, potentially for the full six minutes, the child gets an uninterrupted audience with their parent (how about that attention as a reward for misbehaving!) as they argue about having to stay on the step. Usually the argument is carried out at top volume, and both child and parent are stressed to the hilt by the end of it.

With my approach there is no time limit set on time-out other than the time required for a child to calm down and resume play without misbehaving. When you have instituted a calming time-out for your child in a calm way yourself, then you might find that, within a few seconds, your child is ready to resume normal interaction. If that is the case, then let them resume.

It may take longer for your child to calm down, and that, too, is OK. What sometimes happens, though, is that your child will say they are calm or outwardly appear to be calm. They then get allowed back to whatever activity they had been removed from and go straight back to the misbehaviour. You then have to put them straight back into time-out with the same message about the misbehaviour not being OK and needing to sit apart in the room until they are really ready to be calm. It is OK, too, to say something quickly like: 'You thought you were calm to play but actually you still seem upset because as soon as you went back playing you hit your sister (or whatever was the misbehaviour).'

CHILDREN LEARN NOTHING FROM PUNISHMENT

Parents often ask me, 'That's all very well, but what about punishment? He needs to know, for example, that he will be punished for hitting his sister.' The reality is that your child doesn't need to learn that he will be punished for hitting his sister. He needs to learn that hitting his sister is wrong, unfair, hurtful and unacceptable. You don't get those messages from any punishment, but from a swift response that prevents the hitting from continuing and a verbal message that espouses your values and beliefs about hitting. Punishment just teaches that, if you do 'bad' things, then bad things happen.

For some children the negative consequences or punishments are sometimes worth the infringement! Being made to sit on the step for six minutes might be worth the pleasure of giving a good hard slap to your brother. Such a response from a child is likely to lead to stricter imposition of increasingly severe forms of punishment. All the time what is happening is that the punishment eventually stops acting as a deterrent, and so the old bold behaviour resumes until you can come up with a more threatening punishment. That is a self-defeating spiral of interaction to get stuck into with your child. It is hard, too, after a while to pull back from using threats of punishment as your only source of behaviour management.

COPING WITH SHOPS WHEN YOUR CHILD MUST COME TOO

Going to do the weekly shopping with a toddler in tow can be a nightmare. Supermarkets, by their design, are very stimulating places. There are so many new sights, colours, sounds and smells for your toddler that it's no wonder they get all excited when they go in.

Before we look at what you can actually do if you have to bring your toddler with you, let's look first at the different options you might have for getting the shopping done without your toddler in tow. If there are two parents in your family, it may make sense for one of you to stay at home with the children and the other one to go and do the shopping. I know in our house this is a system that seems to work best. I can run around the shops straight after work, hassle-free and in half the time that it would take if I had my crew along with me.

Another alternative might be to arrange a shopping swap with a friend. You could mind their children while they go shopping and then they could return the favour. You could shop online, if there is somewhere that delivers to your area. If the supermarket or shopping complex has a crèche, it may also be worthwhile investing in your child spending some time there while playing when you get on with the business of shopping. Depending on how big a struggle shopping is for you with your children, you may decide that, whenever you get an offer of help to mind the children, you use that time to get some shopping done.

Of course, not everybody does struggle with shopping with their small children. Some families manage to get into a routine where their children are used to simply trawling around the shop with their parent, they know full well that they are not in line for a treat at any stage and they are also aware that they need to stay calm or else there will be a consequence for them. This is somewhat of an ideal world. It can be achieved, but only after a lot of hard work. Essentially, to get to this stage you yourself have to be calm, focused and determined whenever you go shopping.

TREATS

One of the first decisions you are going to have to make is whether or not you are ever going to buy your child a treat during or after the shopping. Whatever you decide, you then need to stick to it consistently every time you go shopping. It may work for you and your family, for example, to have no treats during the shop but for your children to know that if they have behaved during the shopping there will be a treat for them when you're finished and on the way home.

This uses the sound principle that good behaviour gets rewarded. Of course, you do need to specify what good behaviour entails. This 'good behaviour' might mean, for example, that there is no whining during the shopping and that there is no stuffing of unnecessary items into the trolley. In my experience, both of these can be quite a challenge for the average toddler. Even though shops are generally very stimulating, there is no doubt that small children quickly get tired and bored with the repetition of going up and down the aisles and become far more interested in creating a game of the same task and running riot in the process.

> Supermarkets are very stimulating places. There are so many new sights, colours, sounds and smells for your toddler that it is no wonder they get all excited

Buying them a treat during the shopping is more of a distraction than anything else. Inevitably, it ends up being something like a packet of crisps, a bar of chocolate or a sugary drink. This is not ideal, as sweet treats are a bad habit to get children into. Also, when the treat runs out, you have a sugared-up little bundle of energy with nothing left to lose! If you're treating during the shopping, then you need to shop fast.

GRABBING AND DUMPING

If your child is a compulsive grabber and dumper, i.e., grabbing things from the shelves and dumping them into your trolley, you may want to restrict their movement by either insisting that they keep hold of the trolley all of the time or, if they are small enough, sitting them into the child seat on the trolley. You may decide that your child or children are allowed to pick one luxury or unnecessary item when they go out shopping, and this may satisfy their need to put things into the trolley. Alternatively, you can really engage with your child and keep them busy filling the trolley with the items that you want. It is great if you can make a game out of this, suggesting, for example, that you are both part of a conveyer belt system or getting them, each time, to determine whether the item is heavier or lighter than the previous one. You could also engage them in noticing the items for colour, or texture. You can then challenge them to match the item with items already in the trolley of similar texture or colour. All of these tasks serve to distract your child, hopefully for long enough to get around the shops without them coming demanding and whingeing and taking matters into their own hands.

WORLD WAR THREE AND THE SIX-PACK OF CRISPS

So let's assume that, for whatever reason, neither keeping your child close to you nor distracting them has worked. Your three-year-old has decided that the particular six-pack of crisps that she has plucked from the shelves must come home with you or else her life will be worth nothing. She clings to the bag even as you firmly say 'no'. She clings to the bag even as you warn her that, if she doesn't let it go, you will take it from her and put it back on the shelf and she will lose her treat at the end. Unfortunately, because of her mood, your last warning is like a red rag to a bull, and her sense of injustice that the world is no longer a fair place overrides everything else, and she breaks down into a huge tantrum.

Even though shops are generally very stimulating, there is no doubt that small children quickly get tired and bored with the repetition of going up and down the aisles

Your little daughter, who is normally placid and amicable, is sitting there on the floor of the shop clinging to a six-pack of crisps and screaming and wailing and drawing a crowd. After you have done your few deep breaths to try and hold on to your own anger at the way in which she is both frustrating and embarrassing you, you then need to take action quickly. Firstly, remove the six-pack of crisp from her arms. She is upset already, and the additional upset of not having the bag of crisps is not going to make a huge difference.

It will probably just lead to one extra-loud wail. Then, you need to offer her one chance to calm down before you remove her from the shop. If, as is likely, she has gone past the point of being rational, you then pick her up and carry her out of the shop.

Yes, it does mean abandoning your trolley as you carry her out of the shop. If you can, en route to the outside, try to say to a shop assistant that the trolley is there and you will be back for it. When you get outside, either find a quiet seat or bench somewhere or if you have your own car, go sit in it. This now is the time to use real 'time-out'. Sitting with your child, let them know that when they are calm you can go back and continue the shopping. If the weather is good enough you might want to leave your door open so that your ears don't take too much of a bashing if the crying continues.

Sitting with a screaming child is not easy – let nobody tell you otherwise! It is important, though, for you to be able to suffer through the tantrum without having a tantrum of your own. It is OK to sit quietly, ignoring your child and waiting for the moment that the crying subsides. If you do interact with them, it needs to be with the same message as always: 'When you are calm, we can continue.' As soon as that calmness comes, you need to notice your child and make some positive comment. Something like: 'You have stopped crying, that is great because now we can continue shopping.'

FINALLY, CALM AFTER THE STORM

Assuming that they remain calm and have realized that the whole incident is over and resolved, you go back into the shop, head for your trolley and resume shopping as if nothing had happened. The incident is over and has been dealt with. There is no need for big lectures about not taking crisps, or lectures about appropriate or inappropriate behaviour in shops. When you took your child out of the shop you gave them a very clear message that screaming in shops will not be tolerated, and so they are going to be removed. You need to hold on to this kind of resolve every single time you go shopping with your children. Obviously, it gets more difficult if you have more than one child because, in order to remove one child, you have to bring all of them with you. Any other children, who haven't been having a tantrum, are likely to have their noses well out of joint if they too have to leave the shop with you. You don't really have much option but to rely on their forbearance and goodwill.

> **When you took your child out of the shop you gave them a very clear message that screaming in shops will not be tolerated**

Just as in every situation that I describe throughout the book, your goal is to be consistent and to let your child know at every step along the way that you recognize that they are upset, but when you say something you mean it. What you will probably find is that, if you can become consistent for your child in every other situation, soon they will just stop pushing the limits in the shops because they know that you are going to follow through on whatever consequence, or reward, that you have promised.

KEY POINTS TO REMEMBER

- Most tantrums occur for one of two reasons: your child is frustrated or seeking attention.

- Your response to the tantrums may lead to the attention-seeking tantrums happening more often if your child learns that, by having a tantrum, they get lots of notice (even if that is negative).

- Distraction and diversion work well to avoid tantrums provided you use them early enough before the tantrum gets really fired up.

- Distraction involves either redirecting their energy to another task or doing something that allows them to forget about the source of the tantrum.

- Your key message in responding to a tantrum is that, while you can understand the reason for the tantrum, you can't do anything to help your child until they are calm.

- After you have given this message, you let them have some time-out to calm down.

- Time-out is not a punishment.

- If time-out is used as a punishment, it is the emotional equivalent of slapping.

- When your child is taking time-out to calm down, you need to be alert to any signs of that calming so that you can notice it, praise it and give them attention for being calm.

- There are lots of ways of distracting and engaging children during the shopping, such as involving them in putting things in the trolley and getting them to compare and contrast the items they are lifting.

- If they have a tantrum in the shops or anywhere out and about, you respond to them as you would at home.

- This means being prepared to leave the shop or wherever you are in order to give your child time-out to calm down.

5

DEALING WITH BOLD BEHAVIOUR

WHEN SAYING 'NO' IS NOT ENOUGH

Your children need limits to guide, direct and protect them. Limits are those 'lines in the sand' where we determine what is, and is not, acceptable and appropriate for our children. Limits are those house rules we have.

Sometimes, our children will view limits as a challenge to be overcome. Our children test limits in order to see do we really mean what we say. They test limits in order to experiment with their own power and independence. In testing the limits they often test our patience, and sometimes in the face of the pressure they bring to bear we crumble and give in to them. Invariably, when we set a limit that we don't keep, we make our parenting job harder.

We spend a lot of time and energy worrying about and trying to respond to our children's behaviour. More often than not, we get most stressed when we anticipate that that behaviour is going to be visible and on public show. How we respond to and manage these behaviours is really important, though, because the likelihood of them doing any of those behaviours repeatedly or persistently (when we might begin to see it as a problem) is dependent on our reaction. What I would like you to think about and change is how you react to your child in order to minimize the likelihood of bold behaviour being repeated.

Essentially I am going to focus on the core skills that we all need to manage our children in the day-to-day, when they are not having tantrums but are doing all the other things that we don't like. Yes, this is the time that I am going to harp on about consistency. I'm also going to explain the notion of reinforcement and use it to describe how to respond to your child to decrease the likelihood of the bold behaviours being continued and to increase the likelihood of better behaviours being shown. This chapter describes the essence of my beliefs about general behaviour management.

THIS CHAPTER LOOKS AT ...

What do psychologists mean by reinforcement?

The me, me, me of attention-seeking

Crime and punishment in the pre-school years – how to set limits and stick by them

Catching your child being good – attending to the behaviours you want to see more of

Do children really want to earn stick-on stars? How to use star charts effectively to promote good behaviour

Consistency, predictability, harmony. The Holy Grail of parenting

WHAT IS REINFORCEMENT?

When psychologists use the term 'reinforcements', they are not talking about supporting troops arriving to save the day. Rather, they are talking about things or events that serve to make children's behaviour more likely to occur again. Psychological researchers used the term reinforcement to describe the actions they took to teach animals to learn and unlearn certain types of behaviour. Some of the earliest behavioural experiments were carried out using dogs by a man called Pavlov. You may have heard of Pavlov's dogs.

At its most simple, behavioural theory proposes that, when we take an action that is followed by a pleasant reaction, we are more likely to carry out the original action again. Try it with your two-year-old: wait until they make some spontaneous movement or sound. Immediately laugh and smile at them. The chances are they will do it again immediately, hoping for a similar response from you. Even if you don't respond by

When we take an action that is followed by a pleasant reaction, we are more likely to carry out the original action again

laughing, they may try it a couple more times to see if they can evoke the laugh response from you. If you don't ever laugh in response, they will probably not bother to do the action again. If you laugh every time they do it, they will keep it up for some time.

This process of smiling or laughing in response is you 'reinforcing' the original action (whatever it was). When you respond in the same way every time, we psychologists would term it 'continuous reinforcement'. Continuous reinforcement is a great way of behaviourally 'training' your child that good things come in response to good behaviour.

The curious thing, using the example above, is that, if you only respond by smiling every so often in response to the action, your child will become more and more persistent in trying to do the action to get you to smile or laugh. What you are doing then is termed 'intermittent reinforcement', i.e., you are rewarding the action with a smile or laugh occasionally or intermittently. Intermittent reinforcement is the most powerful kind of reinforcement you can use. When you don't know whether your action will get the desired response or not (but you believe that eventually it will get the response), then you keep doing the action regularly. The addictive nature of gambling works on the basis of intermittent reinforcement. Whether you win or not after placing a bet is unpredictable, but the possibility of winning and the intermittent occasions when you do win make it imperative to keep trying.

To translate this back to the world of children, we often use intermittent reinforcement, unknowingly, to reinforce exactly the kind of behaviour we would like our children to stop. Think of times when you refuse your child a treat because it is too close to dinnertime or because they have had enough chocolate for one day. They respond by having a tantrum because they are so frustrated. Some of the time you can hold fast and not give the treat, remaining firm and resolute with your initial decision. Some of the time, intermittently, however, when you are tired or under pressure, you do

Being consistently firm and holding a limit that you have imposed is crucial

give in and allow the treat (against your better judgement, probably) in order to get a bit of peace and quiet. Unfortunately, what you are doing is giving your child the message 'If you can throw a big enough, distressing enough or loud enough tantrum you might or might not get what you want.' In those circumstances your child will unconsciously decide it is always worth having a tantrum because they might get what they want, and the possibility of getting it by having a tantrum is worth the risk of not getting it by having a tantrum.

The upshot of all this is that you need to pay close attention to the responses you give to your child when they act up. Being consistently firm and holding a limit that you have imposed is crucial. If you give in on your limit, then your child learns simply that you don't mean what you say, and it is always worth the shot of arguing or fighting against your decisions.

ATTENTION-SEEKING

A two-year-old probably believes that the world they inhabit revolves around them. If they were to construct their galaxy they would ensure that they are their own shining sun and the rest of us are the orbiting planets, waiting to meet their every need. After all, when they were babies, inevitably the world as they perceived it probably did revolve around them. Babies have such basic care needs that have to be met by a parent or caregiver that we do end up responding to them according to their timetable. If they seem tired, we invest time in getting them to sleep; if they seem hungry, we will often feed them on demand; if they seem uncomfortable, we will change their nappy.

This belief that the world revolves around you is known as egocentrism. It comes as an awful, albeit developmentally important, shock to the system to realize that actually your mum is not your servant and play companion as and when you decide. This loss of the automatic attention that your toddler got when he or she was a baby is often hard for them to manage. They, therefore, seek to get the attention back by whatever means it takes. If you put yourself into the shoes of your toddler, their need for your attention makes more sense, frustrating and all as it may be for you when you don't have the time to give.

All those parenting books that identify certain children's behaviours as attention-seeking also suggest ways of avoiding and withdrawing attention from your child. Using behavioural principles, those techniques are intended to work on the basis that, by not giving your child attention when they misbehave in an attention-seeking way, it is less

It comes as an awful, albeit developmentally important, shock to the system to realize that actually your mum is not your servant and play companion as and when you decide likely they will misbehave in the same way in the future. In other words, they should be learning that, when they act up to get our notice, they, in fact, get less attention. However, I would argue that in this process of parents ignoring them when they look for our attention they learn that, to get noticed, they have to become more extreme or loud or dangerous or provocative or disruptive in order for adults to respond to them, because the reality for most parents is that they do respond to their children eventually, and their children know this.

I think this basic behavioural principle (of ignoring a child to reduce their attention-seeking behaviour), while correct in theory, needs to be very carefully applied to relationships with children. If we have been able to identify that our children are acting up, maybe by throwing a tantrum, in order to get our attention, then that suggests to me that, rather than getting less of our attention, they need more of our attention. If the only way our sons and daughters can communicate to us that they would like us to pay them more attention is by screaming and banging around the house, then let's translate the message and respond to it. What is required in situations where children seek more attention is to give them more

What is required in situations where children seek more attention is to give them more attention

attention. Of course, it might not be practical or even desirable to give lots of attention suddenly just because your son demands it by his behaviour. So you don't give him the attention in response to the actual tantrum but you do increase the amount of positive attention you give him at other times. So, as I was explaining earlier in the chapter on tantrums, you can translate his behaviour for him during the tantrum and then let him know how you will be responding to it.

For example, you notice that, when you come in from work every evening at 6 p.m., your four-year-old daughter will almost immediately become 'hyper' and start dragging out of you. I'd guess that your usual response would be to start giving out to her and reminding her of all the jobs you have to do, along with all the things she has to do before bed. The more you try to get the space to do the jobs that have to be done, the more she pulls and drags out of you. Finally, it probably reaches a point at which you threaten to put her out on the stairs if she doesn't calm down and give you some space (the dreaded time-out as punishment for bugging you!). You end up cross, and she ends up cross.

Another way of dealing with this situation might be to recognize that her 'hyperness' and clinginess are signs that she has been missing you and would like you to spend time with her so that she can feel reconnected to you after the day. After you have recognized the pattern, you could respond by planning to give the time to her before she has an opportunity to have her attention-seeking tantrum. Allot fifteen minutes (set an egg timer if it helps to keep the limit) for play as soon as you come home. Let your daughter choose the game, and give it your all for those fifteen minutes. As the time to finish approaches, give your child some advance warning of the end and plan for the

If the only way our sons and daughters can communicate to us that they would like us to pay them more attention is by screaming and banging around the house, then let's translate the message and respond to it

next time you will spend time together in an uninterrupted way (maybe story time later, when the dinner has been cooked).

In the early stages of introducing a response like this you will probably find that your daughter will struggle to accept the ending of the playtime, and you will have to remain firm and steadfast in the face of her tantrum. As the days pass, however, you will find that she begins to realize that she can trust you to give her the time and she gets the full time (the egg timer proves it!) that you promised. This consistent and trustworthy behaviour from you will give confidence and security to your child that you follow through. They also get fifteen really good minutes of playtime. This is a real treat for any child. Most importantly, however, the pulling and dragging for your notice and attention will diminish.

It may seem paradoxical, but actually the more time you spend with your child, the

It may seem paradoxical, but actually the more time you spend with your child, the less of your time they will demand. Investing time in them means that ultimately you will get the time and space for yourself

less of your time they will demand. Investing time in them means that ultimately you will get the time and space for yourself.

If you can't respond by giving the time there and then, you need to make a promise to your child that you will set time aside especially for them at some stage in the evening. Try to make the start time obvious for your child. For example, at the end of your favourite soap opera or when the dinner dishes are taken off the table. Just make sure to follow through and begin the playtime whenever you have agreed to do it. Again, you may find that your child will initially struggle to accept that you will actually set the time aside, but a few days of consistency should alleviate that anxiety.

As an aside, this example really reminds me of the importance of developing a routine for the evenings. If your house is like mine, then those couple of hours between getting home and getting children into bed is a fraught and busy time. The chapter on sleep has ideas about how you might want to structure that time. Structuring does help children, as the predictability it creates is both reassuring and guiding for them.

CRIME AND PUNISHMENT

The heading 'crime and punishment' may seem a little extreme and even provocative. However, the reality is that many of us do see our children's behaviours as crimes. Unfortunately, some of the time we also see them as crimes perpetrated deliberately against us. It is as if, sometimes, we see our children's behaviour as their way of intentionally annoying, frustrating and provoking us. The resulting anger that we feel often does indeed provoke an over-reaction from us. There is no doubt that we often do punish our children. Sometimes we dress up punishments in nice language, calling it 'consequences'.

A consequence suggests that it's a natural reaction simply based on cause and effect. It is just us following the laws of physics that state that every action has an equal and opposite reaction. So when we decide to impose consequences on our children all we are doing is giving them a natural response to their own actions. Or are we? It seems to me from the work that I have done with other families and from my experience in my own family that actually what we are doing is punishing our children because we believe that they did wrong or that they were bold. The theory behind our punishing, even if we call it imposing consequences, is based on the behavioural principle that if a bold behaviour from a child gets them punished (i.e., elicits a negative outcome for them) they won't want to do that behaviour again for fear of the punishment.

> Sometimes we dress up punishments in nice language, calling it 'consequences'

Unfortunately, when we apply this particular principle to children's behaviour, we can often, quickly, become quite extreme in the levels of punishment we give to our children. Our children often don't respond initially to the consequences we put in place. Let's say, for example, that you decided to 'ground' your child for an hour because he pushed over another child while he was out playing. You let him back out to play after the hour, and within five minutes he has pushed another child over. You then decide to keep your child in for the rest of the evening. If they push someone the next day, the chances are you will be losing your patience and thinking that the consequences/punishments aren't working and so you increase the level: you ground him for a week.

'A week is a long time in politics,' so the saying goes, and it is also a long time in the life of a three- or four-year-old. What is happening is a mixture of us taking out our own frustrations on our children for not getting the message and us trying to make the consequences/punishments so aversive that our children could not possibly want to behave boldly again. Unfortunately, our children often don't understand that this is the message that we are trying to give. If they do get the message, then maybe the punishment is not acting as a deterrent. But I would caution against increasing the severity of the punishment, because what ends up happening is that some very harsh punishments get doled out to children, all in the name of behaviour management.

> It is not OK to tell your child that they are bold, as this labels your child and will make them feel bad about themselves

CHILDREN ARE NOT BOLD, BEHAVIOURS ARE BOLD

Because our children are human, they can experience those punishments, not just as a 'cause and effect' response to their own behaviour, but as an emotional statement from us. Usually, when we give out to children and impose a punishment for bold behaviour we, very crossly, tell them that they are bold, and so the punishment is such and such. The emotional message our children will pick up is that they are bold, not their behaviour, and so they internalize this boldness. That means that they start to believe themselves that they are bold. Understandably, if you already believe you are bold, then you have nothing to lose by doing bold things.

Children who believe that they are bold because they have been told it repeatedly by their parents and other adults will also, probably, believe that nobody likes or loves them because of this. It is crucial to separate out the child from their behaviour. It is OK to tell your child that they are behaving in bold ways or that a specific behaviour is bold and won't be tolerated. This labels the behaviour. It is not OK to tell your child that they are bold, as this labels your child and will make them feel bad about themselves. It will strip away their self-esteem.

The other difficulty you face in giving extreme reactions to your child for their misbehaviour is that children often will try to ignore the fact that the reaction they are getting from their parents is negative and will be pleased just simply to be getting a reaction at all. That big reactions, punishments included, are directed towards them guarantees that their parent is paying them 100 per cent attention, and in certain circumstances that is enough for any child. They then act boldly to get your attention rather than fear any consequence or punishment.

LEARNING ABOUT THE NATURAL CONSEQUENCES OF BOLD BEHAVIOUR

So what do we need to actually do? We can't get rid of consequences, because children do need to know that there are certain limits, and that when they have reached those limits there will be consequences. After all, this is the way the world works. Cause and effect is a reality. They need to know that certain kinds of behaviour are not OK; they need to know that certain kinds of behaviours hurt and are not acceptable.

I always promote the idea of natural consequences for behaviour. What I mean by this is that the consequence should fit the misbehaviour, both in manner and in scale. For example, if your child deliberately drops food on the floor at dinnertime, then a natural consequence is that they have to clean up the mess (alone if they are old enough, or with your help if they are younger). Other consequences you may like to consider for your children, depending on the context and the circumstances, include:

- Withholding a treat that was due
- Removing some privilege that was expected
- Giving an extra chore (setting the table, for example)
- Making amends by doing something nice for someone you fought with

- Stopping your child from continuing to play where they were
- Restricting access to the television
- Having to hold your hand instead of running or playing freely
- Having to sit in the trolley instead of walking around the supermarket.

With all of these the key to remember is to be reasonable and to only use consequences that seem to fit with the misbehaviour.

Two consequences that I never recommend are sending a child to bed and slapping. Sending a child to bed gives them a negative message about the function of their bed. Bed as a place of punishment could really disrupt their sense of bed as a secure, safe place to sleep at night. Slapping is physical abuse, because parents are bigger, stronger and more powerful than their children. Slapping simply teaches children that, when you are cross and angry (as parents inevitably are by the time they consider a slap), it is OK to hit out at someone. By slapping you are role-modelling hitting.

PUTTING THE THEORY INTO PRACTICE

Let me explain the technique I would use for most social behaviour problems like hair-pulling, biting, fighting, kicking and so on. We'll take the example of your son hitting his little sister. Initially, you give a clear message that the behaviour is not OK ('Hurting is not allowed in our family'). Then you move your son away from the situation, but keep him with you, to give him a chance to become calm ('You need to come with me now until you are calm'). You then tell him that, when he can play without hitting, he can return ('When you are calm enough to play without hitting, then you can go back to the sitting room'). As soon as he seems calm, you let him back to play. If he continues to hit, then you keep removing him with the same messages.

By slapping you are role-modelling hitting

You are using a form of time-out but only to give your child the time to be calmer and more ready to play 'nicely'. By using time-out in this way there is also the consequence for your child that they are removed from their play for a short while until they can demonstrate that they can play without hitting or biting or whatever. Perhaps this may 'teach' your child not to hit, but that is not its purpose. The repetition of your expectation that hitting is not allowed is what will 'teach' your child not to hit.

If you want to bring in a consequence for the hitting, then it would be that your son has to do something nice for his sister to make amends. The nice thing might be to draw a picture for her, to stroke her on the arm where he hit her or maybe to go and play in a different room to give her uninterrupted space to play. These additional consequences may bring home the message that hitting is not nice and is not allowed, and that in your house you like to be nice to each other.

The best way to become reasonable in imposing consequences on our children is to become reasonable in setting the limits in the first place. Setting a limit is when you advise your child of what your expectation of them is. Usually we do this alongside giving them a warning of what will happen if they don't live up to our expectation (the consequence). For example, if you are out for a walk, you may say to your four-year-old son, 'You cannot run off out of my sight (limit). If you do run off then you will have to spend the rest of the walk holding my hand (consequence).' I would consider this to be fair and reasonable, both as an expectation of his behaviour and as a consequence if he fails to meet that expectation.

> The best way to become reasonable in imposing consequences on our children is to become reasonable in setting the limits in the first place

Sometimes, however, our expectations of our children are unreasonable. We expect them to be quiet when it's not possible for them to be quiet; we expect them to be calm when it's not possible for them to be calm; we expect them to eat when it's not possible for them to eat; and we expect them to jump when we have determined how high.

Assuming you have explained the limit and advised of the consequence, before you get to the stage of imposing that consequence it is vital that you have given your child a warning that they are about to break the limit. Sometimes children forget about the limit or they are distracted or frustrated and can't focus on what they should be doing.

You need to refocus them and give them a chance to get their behaviour back on track in a positive way. I often advise my children that I am going to count to three, and if they haven't stopped the misbehaviour by the count of three, then the consequence (whatever it is) will happen. You can then count slowly to three, talking in between to give lots of chances to do the right thing.

So, typically, in the example of the walk, you might say, 'I can see you are running far. Be careful not to go out of my sight. You need to come back closer to me or you will end up stuck by me holding my hand. I'm going to count to three and if you are out of my sight when I get to three you will have to hold my hand. One … You are too far away, come closer … Two … Remember, if you can't see me, then I can't see you, so come close to me … Three … You went out of my sight, so now you must hold my hand for the rest of the walk.' You then ensure that they stay holding your hand. If you use this kind of warning consistently and you always follow through if you get to three, then your children will usually change their behaviour and stop misbehaving by the count of two. The key to it is to be consistent both in giving the warning and in taking action after you have given the warning.

The only times I don't give a warning is if I see one child hurting another child or if their behaviour is dangerous to themselves or others. Swift and immediate intervention is required (as I described earlier) rather than warning and waiting while a child continues to hit his little brother or sister, or wanders into the roadway.

MAKING THE 'PUNISHMENT' FIT THE 'CRIME' – AND MAKING LIFE EASIER FOR YOURSELF

When we set a limit for a child by insisting that they must do something or they must stop doing something, then we can quickly get involved in a battle of wills. After all, if you are telling your child that they must eat their dinner, then you must be able to justify why they 'must'. If they don't eat have they broken a law? Will they die of starvation? The answer to both those questions is probably 'no', and yet we have determined that they must eat. So what are the justifications? Often, in response to a question from a child like 'Why must I eat it all?', we respond 'Because I say so.'

You may snigger to yourself reading this, but I bet you've said it. Sometimes, there is no justification for why we determine something must be a certain way. However, because we have determined that that's how things should be, we then have to try to enforce our will. We usually do this by letting the child know that, if they don't bend to our will, there will be serious and unpleasant consequences for them. 'Oh, if you don't eat it all then there will be no dessert for you.' 'If you don't eat all that, then you are going straight to bed.' 'If you don't eat that now, you will eat it later when it's cold.'

So very quickly what is happening is that, by imposing a particular limit (having to eat), we slip into imposing a string of consequences. So, if we had wanted to avoid all of those consequences, then perhaps we could have avoided setting the limit in the first place. Imagine if you had said at the outset, 'You must eat as much of your dinner as you can.' Wouldn't it have been a different outcome? There would then have been no battle to try to get your child to eat all of the food on their plate, and you

> When you impose a consequence you must follow through and enforce it or you are telling your child: 'I don't mean what I say'

wouldn't have had to impose a string of consequences which you then have to enforce.

And that is another difficulty with the whole idea of consequences and punishments. Once you have imposed a consequence, then you must follow through and enforce it. If you don't enforce the consequence, then all you are telling your child is: 'I don't mean what I say.' The reality is, of course, that usually we do mean what we say but sometimes, in the heat of the moment, we do make threats of consequences that actually are going to be way too hard to try and follow through on.

For example, I have talked to lots of parents who describe grounding their children for up to a week. The result is a disaster and a week of stress. Grounding, as it's generally understood, is the process in which you deny your child the privilege of going out to play. Grounding, by its nature, is a bit of a double-edged sword. Keeping our children in just adds to their frustration, impatience and excess energy. This then gets unleashed upon us, and we often have further episodes of bad behaviour.

The difficulty, in this situation, arises because the parents impose a consequence that actually is unenforceable (being grounded for a week). It isn't realistic for them to expect to be able to keep their child in for a week, nor is it reasonable to expect their child to be able to survive being kept in for a week.

The difficulty could have been avoided if the parents had thought first about how reasonable their consequence actually was. A good litmus test may be to consider how able and willing you will be to follow through and enforce the consequence. If you are prepared to threaten a consequence, then you also have to be prepared to enforce it. You need to be able to see down the line what would be the impact of having to enforce a consequence long before you threaten it.

Sometimes, in the heat of the moment, we do make threats of consequences that actually are going to be way too hard to try and follow through on

Despite our best intentions, when our children act up, we all threaten unreasonably at times. We say things like: 'I will never take you shopping again,' 'There will be no more TV in this house,' 'I am not going to cook for you again,' 'You can just stay in your room for the rest of the night.'

When we have imposed extreme consequences we can often feel virtuous when we enforce them, even though enforcing them might actually be causing more difficulties. The original crime or misbehaviour is often completely forgotten, and no lesson is learned as the attention shifts to the consequence, the enforcement of the consequence and the ensuing power battles that rage over that enforcement.

CATCHING YOUR CHILD BEING GOOD

I think parents are very good at catching their children being bold. We have a highly attuned sense of when our children are misbehaving. Indeed, sometimes we even predict that they are about to misbehave and we proactively warn them of what will happen if they do. Even though I think it is important to respond to children's misbehaviour by setting limits and imposing consequences, I also believe that it's really important to balance that by catching them being good. Catching your child being good is a vital antidote to always being locked in conflict with your child. Catching them being good and praising them is a completely different skill and requires a lot more practice.

Most houses that contain babies, toddlers or pre-schoolers are invariably busy. There are a huge number of things going on all at the one time. There are lots of different needs that have to be met and only a limited amount of time in which to try and meet those needs. As a result, stress levels amongst parents are often very high. Those stress levels get even higher whenever our children misbehave. If they start rowing or fighting with each other, we are into the thick of it in seconds. If our children pointedly refuse to eat, we are engaged in a protracted battle to try and get some food into them. When our children throw their tantrums, we have to respond in order to be able to move on about our daily business. All of this 'managing our children' takes a lot of time and energy. As a result, when they are not being bold or misbehaving, we usually use it as a time to catch up on other jobs and tasks. So, if we are not busy correcting our children we are busy doing

Catching your child being good is a vital antidote to always being locked in conflict with your child

FAIR CONSEQUENCES

If you are going to use consequences to guide your children's behaviour, then the key thing to remember is that the punishment must always fit the crime. If you follow these steps, below, then you may find that you rely less on threatened consequences as your main behaviour-management tool.

★ When you are setting a limit on what behaviour is OK and not OK, are you being reasonable? Is your child likely to be able to keep to the limit or will they definitely break it (are you setting them up to fail)?

★ If you are being reasonable, and your child still misbehaves and goes past the limit, then pause before deciding on a consequence. Always think before you speak (this means staying calm and not reacting from your own frustration – taking time-out for yourself), because perhaps no consequence is necessary and simply removing them from the situation with a clear message is enough.

★ Make sure to give your child fair warning that they are about to break a limit and give them time and help to see if they can avoid breaking it.

★ If you do go on to impose a consequence, is it a fair and natural consequence? Will you be able to enforce it? Will enforcing it cause greater distress and lead to more hassle than the original misbehaviour? Is the consequence going to teach your child that the original behaviour was not appropriate or will it just seem like an arbitrary punishment?

★ Now that you have pondered, it's time to act.

everything else that doesn't involve our children.

You can easily see how this could lead to a situation where our children begin to recognize that the only way that they ever get noticed by us is when they misbehave or when they are bold. When they are being good, we are simply too busy to notice them. The only way to counteract this is to start catching them being good.

We have to make deliberate attempts to notice when they are behaving in ways that we like. We have to comment on that in order to let them know that we have noticed. Praising your child is one way of catching them being good. The key to praising as a tool for catching children being good is to be specific rather than general. If, for example, your son brings his dish from the table to the counter after dinner, you may typically say, 'You are a good boy, thanks.' This is general praise (and certainly welcome). In order to make sure that he knows what he did that we are now praising you need to add in 'You are a good boy for bringing your dish to the counter, thanks.' This is specific praise for the behaviour of clearing his dish from the table. This increases the likelihood that he will carry his dish to the counter next time because he knows that you recognized and praised this the last time.

> So, if we are not busy correcting our children we are busy doing everything else that doesn't involve our children

However, I don't want you to think that generalized praise is not good. You'll remember that I advised you to label the negative behaviour of your child rather than label them negatively ('You did a bold thing' rather than 'You are a bold boy'). This is to avoid your child internalizing a belief that they are bold. With praise, to be general and to label your child 'a good boy' is fine. Wouldn't it be great if they internalized a belief that they are good? Such a belief in their own inherent goodness would be a bolster to their self-esteem.

In actual fact, catching them being good doesn't take a huge amount of energy or effort, it just requires that we are aware of our children and what they are doing even when they are quiet. If, for example, you are in the kitchen, and your child is quietly playing in the sitting room, you need to make a small amount of effort to leave the kitchen and whatever job you are doing, to walk in to them and say, 'You're playing very quietly, that's a great help to me to know that you are busy when I am busy doing other things in the kitchen. Thanks for helping the family by playing quietly.' It may sound a little corny, but I'll bet it pushes all the right buttons with your child.

Essentially, what you are beginning to do is to notice your child more during the good times as well as the bad. You are letting them know that you appreciate when they are good. You are letting them know that it's helpful when they are good. This, then, gives them a sense of value, and that value is attributed to the goodness in their nature. As I have commented earlier, it's so easy to strip your child's self-esteem by constantly harping on about the things that they do badly or the things that they do wrong. This is an opportunity to rebuild your child's self-esteem by letting them know what it is, positively, that you value about them and the things that they do. As I was just saying, you can be sure that, if your child is internalizing the negative things that you say to them and about them, they will also just as surely internalize the positive things that you say to, and about, them.

With praise, to be general and to label your child 'a good boy' is fine. Wouldn't it be great if they internalized a belief that they are good?

STAR CHARTS

Star charts are a visual and tangible extension of catching your child being good. They are a way of displaying, for your child and everybody else to see, the extent to which a 'good' behaviour is being shown by the child. Star charts are a record of the number of instances of that behaviour. Every time the child does the behaviour, they get rewarded with a little sticker star (the kind your teacher may have used on your copies when you did your work well). That sticker gets stuck on a page (chart), so you and your child can quickly see a build-up of the number of times they are doing the 'good' thing.

It may be also that you are using the record to further reward your child when they show the behaviour a certain number of times. For example, every five stars that your child collects earns them a further reward, like special time with you, or something else that would motivate them to earn the stars.

So what does a star chart look like? For the uninitiated, a star chart is simply a piece of paper that is sectioned off across the top with all of the days of the week and down the side with details of the particular behaviour that is being reinforced or rewarded. The illustration is of a very simple star chart just to give you an idea. In this example,

Task	Mon	Tues	Wed	Thurs	Fri	Sat	Sun
Washing hands after using the toilet							
Washing hands before eating							
TOTAL	3	3	4	6	6	7	6

the idea is to promote hygiene by encouraging your child to wash their hands after they have been to the bathroom or before they eat food. So every time that they wash their hands, they get a star which is stuck on to the chart underneath the day that it happened and across from the behaviour that it was.

If you were to use a chart like the one illustrated with your child you could make an even bigger deal simply out of making the chart. You can get them maybe to help you choose colours to do the writing or to draw the lines. Or they may decide to colour in some of the boxes or generally make it more pretty and more fun. As you spend time creating and decorating the chart it's also an opportunity to explain the function of the chart to your child.

In this example, you would be explaining to them that you have noticed that they seem to really struggle to remember to wash their hands when they have been to the bathroom or before they come to eat at the table. As a result, you have decided to help them out. You are going to give them a very small prize every single time that they wash their hands after they have been to the toilet and before they eat. That very small prize every single time is a star.

Star charts are a visual and tangible extension of catching your child being good

So in your explanation you have already managed to explain that this is a kind of competition that they can only win and they can't lose, and that something nice is going to happen for them every single time they do the behaviour that you want to see more of. Now, for some children, just receiving a stick-on star is reward enough. It's amazing how reinforcing getting a star can be. Children love the excitement of both achieving the task and being rewarded with a shiny stick-on star. Other children may choose not to have stick-on stars and may prefer to have other kinds of stickers. If you go into any shop that sells stationery, they usually have a selection of different stickers. The range is

huge, and this might also be a task for you and your child to complete together in your preparation for the chart. If they have been taken to choose the particular kind of stars or stickers that they will receive, then at least you know that it's something that they will want to earn.

So, as I was saying, for some children earning the star is the goal in itself. For other children, older and more worldly wise perhaps, the star becomes simply a counting mechanism on the road to a bigger goal or prize.

KEEPING REWARDS SIMPLE, CHEAP AND MEANINGFUL

In the example of hand-washing, you may have decided with your child that they have to earn five stars before they get a different kind of prize. It doesn't matter if the stars are all earned in the one day or if the five are gathered over a couple of days. The kind of prize you choose is not so important as long as it's motivating for your child. Of course, for something like this, you don't want to be spending a lot of money or spoiling your child with lavish treats. Often the best kinds of rewards or prizes are those that involve your time and your attention. So it could be that every time they earn five stars for hand-washing they get story time with you, or they may get ten minutes' uninterrupted playtime with you, or they may get a hand massage from you. Alternatively, you may decide to give them a thing. Again, that thing should be fairly small, maybe a card if they are into card-collecting (like Pokémon or Yu-Gi-Oh!) or a hair clip or bobbin. The idea is not to start spoiling your child but simply to reinforce and reward the fact that they are now washing their hands regularly.

> Children love the excitement of both achieving the task and being rewarded with a shiny stick-on star

When you are using a star chart, it's really important that the star or sticker is received immediately after the specific behaviour is displayed. In order for your child to learn that good things come with hand-washing the two events need to happen close together. So, if your child comes running in to you saying that they have washed their hands, you need to be prepared to stop whatever else you are doing, go to the stickers and the chart and either put up the sticker yourself or let your child put up the sticker under the appropriate day. If you delay, your child might begin to think that you don't have any faith in the chart, and that it's not worth sticking to, or by the time you get to stick up the sticker your child may have forgotten what it is they are getting the sticker for.

Children like star/sticker charts because they are so tangible and visual. It is a very visible way of reinforcing and praising a particular behaviour that your child is doing. Their good behaviour is obvious not just to you and your child but to anyone else coming into the house, too. The chart should be very noticeable, maybe stuck to your fridge in the kitchen or on the wall of the bathroom, where it will be seen by lots of people.

To further enhance the effectiveness of a star chart you can verbally praise your child, too. So, along with any stickers or stars that are going on to the chart, you should be keeping up the verbal praise as well for your child achieving the new or desired behaviour.

Another reason why sticker charts and star charts can be so effective is because they remind you, as a parent, to give notice to your child. When your child comes running in after washing their hands, the fact that you then stop whatever else you are doing means that your child gets a very strong message that you are attending to them and noticing them because they have washed their hands. So, unbeknownst to you, the real reward for your child may not be the sticker but the fact that you stop, notice them and spend time with them sorting out the sticker on to the chart.

It's really important that the star or sticker is received immediately after the specific behaviour is displayed

CHARTS FOR NEGATIVE BEHAVIOUR – CHANGING THE FOCUS

I only ever use star charts for rewarding and recording positive behaviours. I have seen some people using star charts (or black mark charts) as a way of recording the misbehaviours of their children. When their child misbehaves a certain number of times a particular consequence is put in place. Perhaps this can be effective, because the basic theory is sound, but it seems like a dreadful and very public way of highlighting your child's misbehaviour. When a star chart is used positively, everybody coming into the house and seeing the chart can add a little bit of verbal encouragement to your child for what they are achieving. If the chart is used for misbehaviour, however, then equally everyone will come in and use it to have a go at your child for what they are doing wrong. This then becomes just an opportunity for anybody or everybody to strip your child of their self-esteem.

Star charts, though, can be used to reduce the incidence of negative behaviours. To reduce negative behaviours, all that you have to do is reinforce the absence of that behaviour. So let's take another example. Let's imagine that your four-year-old son has developed a jealous habit of pinching his little baby brother every time that he passes. What you noticed is that typically in an hour he may pinch his little brother between five and ten times. You may then decide that, for a concentrated period over one afternoon, you are

> To further enhance the effectiveness of a star chart you can verbally praise your child, too

going to try to reduce this behaviour. So, you take a three-hour period and break it up into units of fifteen minutes. You then explain to your child that, if he can get through fifteen minutes without pinching his little baby brother, he will get a star. And if he can manage to collect five stars, then he will get whatever small reward you think is appropriate (certainly some dedicated time from you, for him, is likely to be a strong motivator). The benefit of using a system like this is that if, during a particular fifteen-minute slot, your child pinches his brother, then all is not lost. He still has a chance to earn a star in the next fifteen-minute period.

You may find, using a system like this, that actually fifteen minutes is too long and that your child can't hold themselves back for a full fifteen minutes. If that's the case, then set the time period to five minutes. Because, as with all star charts, it's really important that your child gets a sense of accomplishment and achievement early on. They need to feel that they are able to earn the stars. If they feel that they can't earn the stars, then they will quickly lose interest and give up on the chart altogether. They will perceive it as too difficult and not worth the trouble for them. However, if it seems like it's easy enough to earn the stars, then they will be much more motivated to keep trying.

The other thing that you will always need to do with star charts is make sure that the particular behaviour that will get the star is very clearly spelled out both for you and your child. So be really specific in deciding the behaviour. Never have a chart that requires your child 'to be good' in order to earn a star. Who's to say what 'good' is? Your child's interpretation of good could be very different from yours. Equally, you may find that, depending on your mood, certain kinds of things can seem OK when you are in a good mood and yet seem like really bad misbehaviour when you are in a bad mood. This makes it a difficult task for your child to know what is expected of them in order to earn their star.

BE CONSISTENT WITH YOUR STARS

As with all techniques that are based on behavioural principles it's absolutely crucial that you stay consistent once you begin a star chart. Every time the behaviour that you are trying to promote happens, you must reinforce it or reward it with the star or sticker. Equally, if you have promised a particular reward for gaining five or ten stars, then you must deliver on that promise. If you don't, your child will lose faith in the star system, and it will become ineffective.

Lots of parents describe to me that their child is madly interested in the star chart at the start but after a few days their interest in it seems to wane. This is not uncommon, but it is worth taking note of. If your child's interest in the chart is waning, there may be some reasons for it. Perhaps they don't feel that it's easy enough to achieve the star or the reward. Perhaps the star is not reinforcing enough and not motivating enough. Perhaps the behaviour has been so long established that actually changing it becomes very difficult. Perhaps they are not sure, specifically, what they need to do to earn the stars, as the category was too general. To counteract these kinds of difficulties you need to make sure that either the stars or the prizes that the child is working towards are indeed motivating for them and you need to hold on to huge amounts of enthusiasm for the star chart as a way of encouraging your child to stick with it. If you seem glum or uninterested in the star chart, then you can be pretty sure that your child will follow suit. However, if you stay excited

> If you stay excited and enthusiastic and keep reminding them of what's on offer on the star chart, then it's much more likely to hold their interest for longer

and enthusiastic and keep reminding them of what's on offer on the star chart, then it's much more likely to hold their interest for longer. Also, be sure to make it explicit and clear what behaviour they have to show in order to get the star.

Of course, if a problem has been in place for a couple of years, it's going to take a little bit longer to change than a problem that has only been present for a few weeks. The message in this is quite clear: the sooner you begin to try to change a behaviour

that you don't like to see, the easier you'll find it. And also, if you are using a star chart to promote some kind of new behaviour, then you need to keep it in place until that behaviour seems habitual.

In our example of hand-washing you may find that, after a couple of weeks, your child seems to remember regularly to wash their hands. After a further week you notice that, not only do they wash their hands, but they forget to come and tell you that they need a star. This is the time to begin to discontinue the chart. For a little while you may leave the chart in place but not fill it in, relying just on verbal encouragement and praise. If that seems to work, then you will know that there is no more need for the star chart.

If, however, after a day or two of stopping a star chart you notice that your child's behaviour reverts to the old way of doing things, then you need to reinstate the star chart. In general, if behaviour seems habitually good, and if your child has stopped reminding you of the need to be reinforced or rewarded with a star, then you can take that as an indicator that the star chart has done its job. You do need, however, to keep reinforcing the behaviour for your child but you should be able to do that just by praise.

You need to hold on to huge amounts of enthusiasm for the star chart as a way of encouraging your child to stick with it

TASK	M	T	W	T	F
Brush teeth	☆	☆	☆		
Tidy room		☆			
Exercise	☆			☆	
Read					☆

CONSISTENCY OF ROUTINE

I have been asked many times in the recent past for my 'top tips' for parents in managing their children's behaviour. I have often listed the top three, with my tongue in my cheek, as: consistency, consistency, consistency. I am a strong believer in the benefits of routine, predictability and rhythm for children. This is particularly the case for the under-sixes, but it is true also for older children.

I like the idea of rhythm in children's lives because it fits with nature. Nature abounds with rhythm. For example, seasons change rhythmically, and day and night change rhythmically, there is an ebb and flow to nature that cries out to us to enjoin. Predictable rhythms in the way the day unfolds for children then also fit with what is natural. Routines give children comfort because they know what to expect.

When morning comes to your house, how are your children roused? Do they awake themselves and have time to adjust to the fact that a new day is beginning or do they awaken to a call from you? Do they get up and eat then dress or do they dress and then eat? Do they wash every morning? Do they sit in front of the TV or have they time to play before the day moves on and activities beckon? Do they have a time pressure on them or can they take the time as they need it? There are many more questions you could ask yourself just about the mornings in your house. The answers are not so important. What I would suggest is important is that, where possible, the same kind of things happen every day. So, if your child rarely wakes before you (lucky you!), then think about waking them in the same way every day – maybe by opening curtains to let light in and nature take its course or by calling gently and maybe shaking. Again, the particular route you take is less important than that you follow the same route every morning.

> I am a strong believer in the benefits of routine, predictability and rhythm for children

When things change all the time it is very hard to settle down and relax. Think of your own experiences, maybe at work, or when you have lots of tasks to achieve. If the goalposts keep shifting, you can never settle into a pattern; that means that you have to expend more energy on trying to understand the shifting, changing environment, and that adds stress and can be very anxiety-provoking. In fact, take the example of going away on a holiday. Being away is usually great: it's fun, exciting, different and hopefully restful. But how many times have you thought as you arrive back, 'It's great to get away but it's lovely to be home again, too.' Why is it lovely to be back? It is lovely because it is comfortable, and we know it well. We know where everything is and how everything is likely to be. The experience for children is the same. If they can rely on certain rhythms, routines and patterns to their day, then they don't have to think about that and they have more cognitive capacity to invest in exploring their world and developing and growing.

You'll probably have noticed that your child will try to create their own routines, even if you haven't created any around them. Often we term their routines as idiosyncrasies

When things change all the time it is very hard to settle down and relax

– like, for example, the way they will wear just the one pair of trousers for days and days in a row, or the way they like the milk to be poured down the side of their cereal bowl rather than over the top of the cereal. Often their idiosyncrasies are frustrating for us to have to accommodate and hugely frustrating for them if they are disrupted. Their frustrations are born of anxiety, anxiety that the world is not a trustworthy and reliable place to be.

Routine, rhythm and patterns in the life of a child allow them to trust. The trust they develop, that the world is essentially a good and predictable place, allows them to be confident. Once there are safe and predictable boundaries, they can stretch themselves to test those boundaries and to uncover the rest of what the world can offer them. However, if they are faced with too much change and uncertainty, then the world will seem a more dangerous and unpredictable place.

CONSISTENCY OF RESPONSE

Equally important in terms of your child's behaviour is the consistency of your response. A lot of times that parents come to me with concerns about their child's level of tantrums or 'bad' behaviour, what we discover is that parents are unwittingly encouraging and maintaining that bad behaviour by being inconsistent. In these kinds of situations it is usually that a child is so demanding and then throws massive tantrums when they don't get their own way.

We now know that part of their reasoning why they should have the thing is because of their egocentrism, their belief that the world revolves around them. Also, though, they have inevitably been intermittently reinforced. If you remember, this is where they have learned that 'sometimes when I throw a tantrum I don't get it, but if I throw a big enough tantrum, then sometimes I do get it'. Simply because we are human and therefore not perfect, there are times we do give in just for the sake of a bit of peace and quiet. This intermittent reinforcement of their bad behaviour is a bit of a killer on the parenting front. As we discussed earlier, the only antidote to this is consistency and not ever giving in to your child's demands if you have already set a limit.

In my head I always repeat a little mantra: 'Say what you mean and then do what you say.' It sounds straightforward but it's hard to put into practice. The first bit about 'saying what you mean' refers to the need to be clear-headed before you set a limit or before you respond to your child's behaviour. Often our own anxieties determine the limits we set.

I remember being at the beach last summer and trying to work out what was a reasonable area for our children to have to stay within. Of course, it was next to impossible to determine how far across the beach or down to the water was OK. In any case, trying to keep them out of the water was unreasonable anyway. Really what was happening was that I was trying to decide on my own safety zone rather than thinking about their needs. In the end we all agreed that it was fair to expect the children to come and tell us if they were going anywhere other than up and down to the water's edge, and that included going in swimming. After that, it was my and my wife's responsibility to stay aware of where they were, what they were doing and whom they were with. In reality this means, of course, that going to the beach has become more about them and their fun than about me and my fun – unless I negotiated time with my wife to abandon everyone for a quick surf! Putting my own needs second behind my children's needs is the thing I struggle with most as a parent.

Anyway, I am digressing; the point is to demonstrate that you have to take the time to think through limits and to talk about them sometimes with everyone involved. If your child is old enough (four to six years of age), then it is OK, and possibly even a good idea, to include them in the determination of the limits. If they have been part of the decision-making process, they may feel more inclined to adhere to the limits that they have created themselves.

This need to think things through also holds for responding to children's behaviour. I have already talked at length about holding back your own frustrations and breathing to take time-out to allow yourself to respond in a reasoned and reasonable way. If you don't do this, you are more likely to just act out your own frustration on your child and to make completely unreasonable consequences a punishment for wrongdoing. This was the second part of my mantra 'doing what you say'. In order for them to benefit from consistency then they need to know that you are a person of your word. They need to be able to trust you that you will follow through on a promised reward or a threatened consequence.

KEY POINTS TO REMEMBER

With children and their behaviour the basic theory of reinforcement suggests that, if they do something and get a positive reaction, they will do it more.

In contrast, if they do something and get a negative reaction, they should do it less.

These principles do hold true most of the time but only if they are applied consistently.

- Children believe they are the centre of their own universe, as they were when they were tiny babies, and so have to learn that actually the world and other people do not revolve around them to do their bidding.

- This is a painful lesson to learn, and so children often do use their behaviour to seek attention and get back to being noticed.

- In theory, if we ignore them when they seek attention, they should learn not to do the bold behaviour to get that attention but they may also experience us as rejecting them unless we are clear about why we are ignoring them.

- In practice the best response to attention-seeking is to understand that we need to give our child more positive attention at other times.

- The more we notice our children, the less attention they seek from us.

- It is important to set limits on children's behaviour – they do need to know that some things are OK and some are not.

- Only using the threat of consequences for not keeping to the limits is dangerous as it sets in place a pattern of ever-more harsh punishments to deter our children.

- Inconsistent application of consequences leads to more of the bold behaviour, as our children can't trust us to remain true to our word.

- Setting limits and imposing consequences must be balanced by catching our children being good.

- The antidote to threats is rewards for good behaviour, and star charts are a very visible way of recording those rewards.

- Star charts are best used to reward positive behaviours.

- Being consistent and predictable makes dealing with children's behaviour much easier.

- When in doubt 'say what you mean and then do what you say'.

6

GETTING YOUR CHILD TO SLEEP

IF ONLY OUR CHILDREN CAME WITH A SNOOZE BUTTON...

Most of us parents will have had first-hand experience of babies' and children's night-time wakefulness. Indeed, at times, it makes a mockery of the phrase 'sleeping like a baby'. Having disrupted sleep is the bane of many parents' lives, and the ensuing tiredness is a frequent cause of shorter tempers and snappier responses both for you and your child. The good news is that we understand the patterns of sleep quite well now, and there are strategies that work to calm the most fretful of night-time wakers. The bad news is that, like most interventions, it requires effort, patience and consistency.

Whenever I talk or write about sleep and bedtimes I am reminded of a friend of mine who explained to me that in his house when he was growing up there were no bedtimes. His parents were night-owls and would commonly be awake until 2 or 3 a.m. He and his siblings would just keep going at night until they fell asleep, either by choosing to go to bed if they felt tired or by just stopping long enough for sleep to overcome them, wherever that occurred. I retell this anecdote to reassure you that, while sleep and your child might seem like a big deal and might be very frustrating for you, there are actually no hard and fast rules. My friend, he and I would agree, is a very well-adjusted adult and bears no scars from his night-times as a child! What I am putting forward below as a suggested approach to sleep remains just that: a suggestion. If it works for you and your family, that's great; if it doesn't, don't despair. Whatever you are doing, as long as you and your child are happy, is good enough.

I have lots of ideas for you to assist your child to sleep. In reality most of us have unrealistic expectations of our children's sleeping, but I know from experience that, if our children don't sleep, then we don't either. It is important, therefore, to maximize our own chances of getting a good night's rest.

THIS CHAPTER LOOKS AT ...

> **The rhythms of sleep**

> **Typical child sleep habits**

> **Promoting good sleep habits**

> **Bedtime routines. Remember that children love predictability. Good habits for the preparation for sleep lessen the likelihood of disturbed sleep during the night**

> **Responding to your waking child**

> **Dealing with nightmares**

RHYTHMS OF SLEEP

You can get through life thinking that sleep is a sedentary and passive state. After all, we are just lying there, aren't we? Well, the answer is yes and no. We are certainly just lying there, but sleep is not passive. Sleep is an active process that changes through the course of the night and follows a particular rhythm and pattern. Even the fact that we generally sleep during the night and are awake during the day is due to a rhythm that our bodies instinctively fall into. That day/night rhythm is called a circadian rhythm.

Because of how humans have evolved over the millennia we have got used to being awake during the day because this is the most productive time. Our eyesight is not well developed for night vision, and so the night-time is potentially a dangerous time for us (certainly in the past, when we were more likely to be caught as food rather than to catch food in the dark). During the day we achieved much more and so we adapted our senses to function better in the day, and so our daily rhythms also evolved to make us more alert in the day and sleepier in the night.

Modern life, of course, means that some people have to work in the night and sleep in the day, and lots of people on shift work will say that the adjustment is temporarily difficult, but as long as they then stay in a night-work pattern, their bodies and brains can adapt. It is if they switch back to a day shift that they struggle again to readjust their circadian rhythm. Air travel has also led to difficulties with circadian or daily rhythms for people. Changing time-zones and suddenly having an extra five or six hours in the day is a shock to the system. That shock has become known as jet-lag and refers to the difficulty establishing a new circadian rhythm to fit with the new daytime/night-time cues we get from our new location. When you hear people talk about their body-clock, they are referring to their own circadian rhythm, the rhythm that tells them about waking and sleeping. If your body-clock and the actual clock are at variance, then you will feel disrupted.

Sleep is an active process that changes through the course of the night

HOW WE SLEEP

Not only does our day/night wakefulness follow a rhythm, but once we are asleep, we follow a rhythm also. Falling asleep is not an event, it is a process. You will probably have noticed, for example, that just before we sleep we become drowsy, and even though our eyes might be open, we are not aware of much that is going on around us. If someone calls our name, or we get disturbed in any way, we can quickly be fully alert again. As we actually fall asleep, we don't instantly reach a point of deep sleep; rather, it is a gradual process characterized by less and less brain activity.

There are two main states of sleep – 'quiet' and 'active' sleep. Quiet sleep, properly known as non-REM sleep, is the kind of sleep that we all typically expect. It is a state of sleep during which brain activity reduces. During the deep states of non-REM sleep, blood supply to the muscles is increased, energy gets restored, tissue growth and repair occurs and important hormones are released for growth and development.

We don't stay in that deep-sleep state continuously, however. After a period of time being deeply asleep we move back up into less and less deep sleep. We then come to a state of almost wakefulness. This state is called 'active' sleep or, more correctly, REM sleep. It is so called because, although our eyes are closed, they are moving rapidly under our lids, hence the name Rapid Eye Movement (REM) sleep. During REM sleep our brain is effectively awake, as, when measured, the amount of activity going on is almost equivalent to a fully awake brain. REM sleep is the period when we dream. You may also notice, if you look at your child during REM sleep, that their heart rate and breathing are irregular. This is normal!

The rhythm, or cycle, from being awake, going down into deep sleep and back into REM sleep takes anywhere between about forty-five minutes (for most babies) and ninety minutes (for most pre-schoolers). Obviously, then, during a typical ten–twelve-hour night sleep period, a toddler is going to have several of these cycles. Also during the 45–50-minute cycle, most tiny babies will spend half their time in non-REM and REM sleep respectively. By about six months of age that has shifted to 70 per cent non-REM and 30 per cent REM sleep during each cycle.

CHILDREN DON'T LIVE BY WHAT THE CLOCK SAYS

This variance between actual clock and body clock becomes meaningful for children at the summertime/wintertime clock change. Gaining or losing an hour in the day often takes weeks for children to adjust to. This is because we adults use the clocks around us as cues to decide about tiredness or wakefulness as well as the light and dark. Small children can't read clocks and so they don't get the additional indicator from the time that we do. Children will not be physically or rhythmically ready to wake up or go to sleep an hour later or earlier, depending on the hour change that has occurred. It takes that extra few days or weeks for their bodies to adjust to a new circadian rhythm.

In fact, since having children, I get bugged by all those people who crow on about how they had their extra hour of a lie-in at the wintertime change. My children have never taken that hour lie-in, and consequently neither have we, their parents!

Because the under-sixes can't read clocks the easiest way for them to regulate their systems is by relying on the light and dark of the day and night. Darkness alone will indicate to your child that it is time for sleep. They also require us, their parents, to regulate their systems and rhythms for them. However, the presence or absence of daylight gives their bodies such strong cues about

> Because the under-sixes can't read clocks the easiest way for them to regulate their systems is by relying on the light and dark of the day and night

being awake or asleep that we have to realize that sometimes these cues are going to supersede our efforts to regulate their rhythms by routine bedtimes, for example. The incongruity of a summertime sun shining brightly at bedtime can be a tricky one for children to accommodate. A blackout blind or curtain becomes a godsend during an Irish summer, as it will lull your child into a false sense that it is darker, and their natural rhythms are more likely to kick in.

Surprise, surprise, almost every parent will tell you that their child is much harder to get to bed and finds it harder to sleep at their usual time during the summer months. (This is also partially linked to the absence of the usual daily routines during the summer, too, but more of this anon.) We need to take account of the circadian rhythm, therefore, in planning children's bedtimes.

I remember on car journeys all of our children used to fall asleep (and still do at times!). If it was a night-time journey, we used to take advantage of this and try to move the children, asleep, from the car to their beds. The depth of their sleep was an important factor in determining the success of the transfer from car to bed. If, for example, they had only just fallen asleep as we approached the house we would often let them sleep on in the car for ten or twenty minutes before trying to move them, knowing that, over the course of those minutes, they were going more and more deeply asleep. If we moved them too soon, they sometimes woke up because they were semi-alert anyway. If we left it too long, they could have moved through their non-REM stage and into REM sleep, where, again, shifting them from the car was likely to wake them. Successfully transferring them from car to bed always felt like such a bonus to our own night, as the whole routine of bedtime and the time and effort involved in helping them to settle was averted. Of course, the time was often filled with unloading and unpacking after the trip instead – otherwise parenting might get too easy!

Difficulty falling asleep and resistance to going to bed are much more common in toddlers. The independence that they are naturally beginning to assert shows itself in a desire to determine their own sleep times

TYPICAL SLEEP HABITS

For all my discussion of circadian rhythms you will have found that your newborn doesn't follow any particular pattern at all. This is because their sleep/wake cycle has to interact with the need to be fed, nurtured and changed. In reality there is no typical sleep pattern for a baby. Newborns will sleep for between ten and a half and eighteen hours a day but on a very irregular schedule. Their periods of being awake can last for anything from one to three hours, and their sleeping periods can be anything from a few minutes to a few hours. You will notice, too, that they seem very restless in their sleep: twitching, moving their arms or legs and sucking.

When babies get a little bit older, between four and twelve months of age, they have usually started to move into more of a night-time sleep pattern. Typically, by six months of age many infants will not need to feed throughout the night (although many, especially breastfed, children will choose to do so) and so are more likely to sleep. By nine months of age that has risen to 70–80 per cent of infants. Most infants will sleep for between nine and twelve hours at night and will also go for between one and four daytime naps that can last for between thirty minutes and a couple of hours.

A blackout blind or curtain becomes a godsend during an Irish summer, as it will lull your child into a false sense that it is darker, and their natural rhythms are more likely to kick in

By the time your child reaches toddlerhood (between one and three years of age), they typically need between twelve and fourteen hours' sleep in a 24-hour period. That means that they will usually drop to one daytime nap (of anything between one and three hours) and then get the rest of their sleep at night. By this stage you will definitely notice that, if they sleep late in the afternoon, it is harder for them to fall asleep at night, and any sleep routine is likely to be disrupted if they snooze late in the day. I always used to try to judge car journeys to fit with our children's nap times, because there was nothing worse than having to travel at about 5 p.m. knowing that they were likely to sleep and then not feel tired again until way past bedtime.

Difficulty falling asleep and resistance to going to bed are much more common in toddlers. The independence that they are naturally beginning to assert shows itself in a desire to determine their own sleep times. Even the fact that they can get out of their bed or cot means they can have more control. With their developing imagination they become more prone to night-time fears and nightmares, too. Toddlers often experience separation anxiety, and that anxiety can also be felt going to bed.

By the time your child is between three and six years of age they are likely to be sleeping for between eleven and thirteen hours at night, and most will drop their daytime nap by the age of five, with many dropping it sooner. Nightmares will become even more common, and they could also develop sleepwalking habits. You should find that keeping them in a routine means that getting them to bed at night is easier (but that all depends on how early and how well you have managed to establish a routine).

Toddlers often experience separation anxiety, and that anxiety can also be felt going to bed

I know the temptation is always there when you get this information about 'normal' sleeping patterns to try to judge where your baby or child is. If they don't seem to be doing what is 'average', you may be a little worried or distressed. However, even if your child isn't falling into the category of 70–80 per cent of the infants who sleep through the night, or your toddler doesn't sleep for twelve hours at night, then don't worry; you are definitely not alone (at the very least there are 20–30 per cent of parents whose infant also doesn't sleep through the night, and that's a lot of parents!). In the next section I look at all the things you can do to promote good sleep habits for your child.

PROMOTING GOOD SLEEP HABITS

So let's look quickly at how you can promote the sleep of newborn babies and infants. The first thing to do is to look for signals that your baby might be feeling tired or sleepy. Some babies will fuss or seem agitated, some may even rub their eyes, and others will cry. Usually after a period of weeks, you can begin to tell the difference between the cries that your baby makes. For example, a hunger cry may have a different tone and intensity to a tiredness cry, and a cry for company may sound different again.

Of course, when it comes to tiredness, your baby may not fuss, rub their eyes or cry. They may have their own unique indicator. And sometimes you just have to judge it by the length of time that they're awake. When they are a little bit older, that fussiness can often turn to crankiness, and you may notice that, if they seem more easily upset, it is probably because they are tired. A good example of that is when you are playing a game where you are bouncing your baby on your knee, and initially they are very happy and giggly, but then after a while the bouncing leads to crying. It's a sign both to stop and probably that your baby is getting tired.

As they move into toddlerhood and pre-school age, children's tiredness is often best judged by their behaviour. Like everyone they will yawn as they get tired, but more often than not you will be seeing increased fractious behaviour, more whingeing and more opposition. Small children are not good judges of their tiredness level and like a wind-up toy they will often keep going until they suddenly drop. If you miss the initial signs of tiredness, or for some reason you can't respond to them (because you are out, for example), you will notice that they can get a second wind. This false energy can keep them going physically, but emotionally and intellectually they are often exhausted and as a result do not cope well with any challenge to their own intentions and become much harder to handle. Trying to settle a toddler in the middle of their second wind is

Small children are not good judges of their tiredness level and like a wind-up toy they will often keep going until they suddenly drop an onerous task and best avoided if at all possible.

Once you have recognized the signs for your baby or child that they are tired, you can then do a range of things to promote their sleep. The first and most important thing is to develop a simple, but consistently used, bedtime routine. I go into some detail in the next section about a typical routine that you may like to try.

Having a strong daily routine and rhythm also helps. Babies and children feel more secure if they know what to expect. You will be taking advantage of the circadian rhythms that I spoke about earlier if you fill the days with predictable but active tasks. This includes making sure that your child gets plenty of fresh air and physical activity. This is especially a challenge in the winter, but even a short walk, cycle or playtime outside can help children. Then, in the evening and at night, make sure that you keep the lights dim as bedtime approaches to get the best value from nature.

Other things to do include using soft music or massages close to bedtime. Check to make sure there are no obvious distractions for your child, like loud music or noisy traffic through an open window. Ensure that they are comfortable in their bed; children can often be too hot or too cold and are not necessarily able to identify this for themselves or us. Some children like to use a comforter at night. In psychology terms this is called a 'transitional object'. It is something that helps them to make the transition from being with us to being on their own. As they move from the secure safe place with us to the 'unknown' place they bring this thing with them, and it reminds them that some things haven't changed. Something like a comfort blanket or favourite toy or teddy can be helpful in providing a bit of security to your child when you are not there.

KEEPING IT ALL CALM AND SOOTHING AT BEDTIME

If you are feeding or changing your baby at night, then remember to keep the lights as dim as possible and to offer as little stimulation as possible to your baby. Avoid talking or chatting with them, as this will only encourage them to become awake and engaged.

Other things to avoid at bedtimes are putting your child to bed with sugary drinks, fruit juices, milk or formula in a bottle. Water is OK, but the others can cause really bad tooth decay. Also, contrary to common belief it is not a good idea to fill your baby with solid food before sleep. This is especially the case if they are younger than six months of age. Their tummies are not able to properly digest the food, and so their sleep may

Also, contrary to common belief it is not a good idea to fill your baby with solid food before sleep

be worse due to a tummy ache that they can't even tell you about. Stuffed-full-of-food babies do not sleep better. You'd be amazed also at the impact that caffeine can have on children's sleep. Hot chocolate, tea, cola and chocolate all have caffeine in them and all can disrupt your child's sleep, even if they are consumed early in the day.

Television and computer games are incredibly disruptive for sleep. If your child watches a lot of TV during the day (more than one to two hours), you may well see it reflected in poorer sleep. Some parents send their children to sleep with a TV on in the bedroom. This is a disastrous habit to develop. Televisions in bedrooms should be banned. Watching television at bedtime is linked to worse sleep. TV stimulates a

If you have a TV in your child's bedroom then remove it, today!

child's mind instead of calming and resting it. When a child falls asleep with a TV on in the background it means that exhaustion, not a soothing or settling experience, has overcome your child and led them to sleep. If you have a TV in your child's bedroom then remove it, today!

BEDTIME ROUTINES

A good bedtime routine is half the battle when it comes to getting children into bed without hassle. Routine, as it suggests, is like a well-worn habit that you and your child both know, expect and, actually, rely upon. As you may have guessed from the explanation above about sleep and circadian rhythms, a bedtime routine doesn't just occur. It must be planned and developed. Unless you guide and direct a routine your child will rely on the cues from the environment, and those cues may be telling them it is still a sunny day, don't stop now!

By developing a routine for the evening and night-time, though, you begin to give your child another set of cues that bedtime is approaching and, from habit, they will begin to settle to the new cues.

First, let's work out a routine that'll work for your family and then let's discuss how to implement it. The first thing you decide is: what is the time you want your child to be in bed and ready to sleep by? If that time is 7.30 p.m., then the routine will need to start at about 7 p.m. I would encourage you to get your child to bed as early as is feasible because small children need lots of sleep.

Typically, don't forget, babies will sleep for about fourteen to sixteen hours a day (not all of it at night!). The average four or five-year-old will need eleven to twelve hours' sleep a day. This must be achieved at night, as it is unlikely they will be napping during the day. Indeed, if you want them to be more likely to sleep in the night, then I would ensure that they haven't napped in the day. If you are waking your child at about 7.30 a.m., then, typically, they need to be in bed, and asleep, by 8 p.m. the previous evening. In that circumstance having them in bed by 7.30 p.m. would be ideal because it will still take your child a short time to actually fall asleep. I know real life is not like a plan, but it is important to have a target time to aspire to. Without it, it is very difficult to develop your routine. Once you begin to implement a routine, though, you will find that your child will accept what might be an earlier bedtime.

THE REAL MEANING OF 'QUALITY TIME'

In choosing the bedtime the other balancing factor might be the amount of time you have managed to spend with your child. If you have been working all day and are only getting home at 6 p.m., then you may not want to start bedtimes an hour after you come in the door. Depending on what you like or need to do when you get in, you may also not be able to start at this time. Think about your own evening and then think about what your child wants and needs. You deciding to have three hours in the evening with them, for example, may seem great, but in fact it is highly likely that you won't actually spend those three hours with your child. You and your child will miss opportunities to spend time together because you are doing other household jobs or are catching up on stuff of your own. Lots of parents will have the TV on and will want a little chill-out time to watch their favourite soap opera. This is not 'quality time' with your child. Rushing around trying to get a load of washing out of the machine and refilling it and folding or ironing clothes is also not 'quality time'. You can certainly make it more child-friendly by including your child in the tasks with you, but sometimes that is not feasible, or it isn't the kind of time that your child wants with you. Also, your child will be getting tired and cranky, like you, the later you are both up, and the possibilities for toddler melt-down will increase dramatically.

> If you put your child's needs first, then you might find that, actually, one and a half hours of your time in a concentrated way is better than stringing the evening out

If you put your child's needs first, then you might find that, actually, one and a half hours of your time in a concentrated way is better than stringing the evening out.

UNDERSTANDING YOUR CHILD'S BODY CLOCK

The other issue that often clouds parents' judgements about the best bedtime is the apparent rhythm of their child who just never seems tired and doesn't appear to be ready for bed at 7.30 or 8 p.m. I called it an apparent rhythm because the chances are that a child not being tired late in the evening is probably just a habit that you have got into with them. For example, you may find that you are only getting your three-year-old daughter into bed at 10 p.m. because before that she just doesn't seem tired enough and will only cause havoc in the room if put to bed earlier. In the morning, she probably sleeps until at least 9 a.m. If you have to wake her earlier to get to crèche or pre-school, then I'll bet she wakes up cranky and bad-humoured.

Your task then is to shift her waking time forward by incremental steps of about twenty minutes at a time over a two-week period. By the time you have got her used to being awake at 7 a.m., you should find that she is naturally more tired earlier the previous evening. Depending on your morning routine, your child being awake earlier but fully rested may actually be a blessing. Shifting the start of bedtime is, I would suggest, just a case of shifting your perspective and your beliefs about how your child will respond.

THE NIGHTLY RITUAL

Let's assume you have picked your time, 7.30 p.m., as the ideal for bed. The things you may want to include in the bedtime routine then are:

- Supper
- Pyjamas
- Teeth
- Hair
- Face
- Cuddle time
- Story
- Bath (optional)
- Foot rub (optional)
- Tales of the day (optional)

Depending on when your child last ate, supper is a good idea before bed. It ensures that your child has enough food not to be disturbed by hunger pangs and they won't wake up starving and cranky because of it in the morning. Always look for balance, though, because too much food late at night means that digestion rather than hunger may be the cause of the disturbance. Be sensible too; don't let supper be full of sugar or E-numbers. This includes the drink they get. Juices and fizzy drinks are a bad idea, especially if they get to bring their drink to bed. After their teeth are brushed you don't want them drinking sugary drinks through the night.

After supper they are either heading for the bath if you are including it, or for their pyjamas and a bit of cleansing. For small children and babies, baths are a great way of interacting in a calm and nurturing way, and the warmth is generally soothing for children, especially if a warm and soft towel is waiting at the end. If you are doing bath as part of the evening routine then stay with your child throughout it, even if they are old enough to be left for periods of time. Washing your child is a very sensuous task and is another way to develop a relationship based on caring, comforting and nurturing. Be slower and gentler in your movements than normal. Use the bath time as an opportunity to massage your baby or toddler, either in the bath with soapy hands or after drying using baby or olive oil. If you can get away without washing their hair then it may be best avoided, especially if it normally induces screams and complaints.

Closeness and intimacy will meet your child's need for attention and, in theory, will mean that they won't need to keep demanding your attention when the lights are out

From bath it is into pyjamas, then hair-brushing and teeth-brushing. Move straight from the bathroom to bedroom after teeth-brushing. If you want to include a foot-rub (assuming you haven't already massaged your child at bath time) or tales of the day then this is the time to do it. Foot-rubbing and you and your child reciprocating tales of the day are about creating opportunities for closeness and intimacy between you. Closeness and intimacy will meet your child's need for attention and, in theory, will mean that they won't need to keep demanding your attention when the lights are out.

Story time also fits the bill for attention-giving and creating a sense of shared intimacy. If you are going to read a story, and I would strongly encourage reading or creating a story for your child every night without fail, then make sure that the book is already in the bedroom waiting. You don't need an excuse for your little boy to run downstairs to go and pick a book! Book-picking is a pre- or post-supper task.

As you read the story, don't get hung up on your child having to be lying down or not interrupting. Story time is story time and not sleeping time, so it is OK for them to be sitting up looking over your shoulder at the pictures or asking questions. The story can be interactive. It is much better to keep interacting and responding to your child than to start getting cross or tetchy because you feel you can't read the story. Getting cross will wind things up rather than helping to wind things down.

As you read the story, don't get hung up on your child having to be lying down or not interrupting

When you finish the story, give your child a last kiss or stroke on the head and then turn off the light and leave them with a final 'Night, night.' Don't be tempted to hang around or wait outside the door. It just lets your child know that you are somehow unsure about leaving them, and they will pick up on this and will definitely call for you. Don't be at all surprised, either, if it then takes your child some time to actually fall asleep. It is not unrealistic to expect them to talk or sing to themselves as they settle to sleep. If they share a room, then they will definitely talk to their brother or sister. Unless the tempo is rising with voices rising too, then it is OK to ignore this. In the next section we are going to look at what to do if your child struggles to settle to sleep from the start or wakes up in the middle of the night and then can't get back to sleep.

RESPONDING TO YOUR WAKING CHILD

I can remember as a new parent one of the most commonly asked questions of me regarding my son was 'Does he sleep the night for you?' I used to hate getting this question because initially I never knew how to answer. If I said 'no' (the truth), then I got a look of sympathy, as if I must be tormented by this little demon who, God love him, wasn't able to sleep through the night. If I said 'yes', then it meant having to lie, but the response from everyone was a sage nodding and a comment to the effect that this meant he must be a great baby.

To my mind there are a couple of assumptions that underlie this question. The first is the assumption that sleeping through the night is a good thing for a tiny baby to do. The second assumption is that my son's sleeping behaviour is somehow an activity he performs for my benefit. I used to hate the inference that, if he didn't sleep through the night without waking, he must be a 'bad' baby or that he must be out to disrupt me.

Of course, research tells us that it is not good for small babies to sleep uninterrupted for too long. Small babies have small tummies and burn up the nutrients from their milk quickly. As a consequence they need to be awake to feed on a regular basis, and this includes being awake at night. The other fact is that disturbed sleep for children is probably more common than we are led to believe.

In the first instance we know that during the REM sleep time many of us, children included, actually come to wakefulness. For most of us, though, unless we need to get up to use the bathroom, we are unlikely to remember being awake because our brains efficiently drift back into sleep without real disturbance.

Small children, though, sometimes haven't learned the art of soothing themselves back to sleep and so, if they come to wakefulness, they often can't drift back to sleep and they call out for Mammy or Daddy. In sleep parlance this is known as 'signalling'. These are the moments that every parent dreads – getting disturbed in their own sleep.

Of course, research tells us that it is not good for small babies to sleep uninterrupted for too long

Indeed, many parents get exhausted and then get upset or angry when their babies and small children wake at night. This is partly due to the strain of having disrupted sleep and having to get up to go into another room to settle their crying child and partly due to our unrealistic expectations that children 'should' sleep through the night.

Hopefully now, if you recall all that we now know about the rhythms involved in how children actually sleep, you can be more tolerant. It is nature that brings them to wakefulness, and what they need from you is to be helped to settle back to sleep.

IT'S GOOD FOR YOUR CHILD TO SLEEP WITH YOU

In our society and culture we have grown to believe that children should be given their own room away from us and they should sleep alone and without support from us. The question 'Does he sleep through the night for you?' is a constant reminder of the desired status quo and a constant prod to go with what society and culture are currently promoting. It wasn't always this way. In our society in the past and in many other cultures and societies to the present it was unheard of for children to sleep alone. Most children slept with their parents or at the very least with their siblings. Co-sleeping, as it is called, was the norm rather than the exception.

> It is nature that brings them to wakefulness, and what they need from you is to be helped to settle back to sleep

As may be clear from how I talk about children, I am a believer in child-centred parenting; taking our cues and guidance from our children about their readiness for different developmental events. I believe we should be focused on their needs and use their feelings as an indicator of need. This is also my view about night-times and sleeping. I think it is good for children to sleep with their parents, especially when they are small babies. I think it promotes security, attachment and confidence. As a bonus, many small children and parents sleep better when they sleep together.

Babies, if they wake and cry, can be responded to instantly, rather than become distressed as a parent struggles to get up and stagger through the house to find and comfort them. If they are in the bed with you, you can settle them to sleep more quickly.

There is no developmental reason why we shouldn't share a bed with our babies and toddlers. Sometimes parents can fear that they will never have their bed back to themselves, but I don't know of any families whose fifteen-year-old still wants to sleep in their bed. The fear of setting up 'bad habits' often leads parents to assume that they must stick with our culturally promoted solo sleeping. But if you start asking around, amongst your friends with children, you'll find that lots of other families vary from the accepted norm at night-times.

However, whether your child sleeps with you or not, you still need to be ready to help them to fall asleep and to respond to them when they are awake. Some experts will say that, starting when they are a baby, it often helps to settle them in your arms, maybe feeding them, maybe just rocking them until they seem drowsy but are not yet asleep, before placing them in their cot or wherever they sleep. Ideally, then they will

I think it is good for children to sleep with their parents, especially when they are small babies. I think it promotes security, attachment and confidence

actually drift off from the point of drowsiness to sleep themselves without the sensation of being held, cuddled or fed and so they will learn that falling asleep is their own responsibility. They will be learning to self-soothe to sleep. It is argued that, as they grow, they are less likely to be a 'signaller', looking for your help to fall back asleep if they wake, as they will be used to falling asleep alone. This is the ideal that many parents aspire to.

The trouble comes when most of us find that our contented and drowsy child becomes very distressed when put down and doesn't just easily drift off to sleep. Instead of remaining drowsy and calm, they start to cry and scream. What do you do then? Some would say you just leave them and let them cry themselves to sleep (yikes!). Others will promote the idea that you pick them up and settle them again to drowsiness and then leave them, and, if they cry, you wait for a slightly longer time before settling them back to drowsiness (yikes!). Others will say that you should pick them up and let them fall asleep in the comfort of your arms or wherever seems safe and secure for your baby. I would always choose the last option for a number of reasons.

I am well aware that developing an independent sleeper for the whole night seems to be the goal for many parents and families, and it certainly seems to be a cultural thing to have children sleeping on their own from as early an age as possible. But my view is that this is not necessarily the best thing for babies and children and not necessarily a goal to aim for. Most babies and toddlers up to about the age of three will experience some level of anxiety when separated from their parents. So up to the age of three you can expect your child to express that anxiety by getting upset. This is true during the day and during the night.

Because that separation anxiety fades in children as they get older you will find that their need to be reassured when they wake at night will also diminish naturally as they get older. Almost all children will have grown out of the need to be reassured if they wake by the age of three or four years, and many will grow out of it sooner. That, of course, is assuming that they have been reassured up to then and not abandoned to cry.

Most babies and toddlers up to about the age of three will experience some level of anxiety when separated from their parents. So up to the age of three you can expect your child to express that anxiety by getting upset. This is true during the day and during the night

REASSURING FRETTING INFANTS HELPS MAKE THEM SECURE AND CONFIDENT

All through this book I have promoted the importance of being aware of, and responsive to, your child's feelings, and this doesn't stop at night. As a direct consequence, I prefer to have babies and children fall asleep in the least emotionally stressful way possible. That means that, when your baby seems tired, fussy and restless, you actually begin to invest more in helping to soothe them. I think it's perfectly OK to rock, cuddle or feed your child to sleep. Yes, it does mean that your child might take longer to learn to fall asleep independently but it's much more likely that they will be secure in their attachments when doing so.

Infants and small children are more likely to develop and maintain secure attachments when their distress is responded to promptly, consistently and appropriately. In other words, when you get up to your child if they cry at night and help to soothe them by whatever gentling methods you prefer (holding, rocking, stroking their head, humming, holding their hand and so on), you will be teaching them that you can be relied

Secure attachments in infancy lay the building blocks for life-long emotional and psychological health

upon to respond to them. You also teach them that their world is essentially a good, safe and reliable place – this is the security that they build into their relationships with you and others. Secure attachments in infancy lay the building blocks for being an emotionally and psychologically healthy child and later adult. If you respond promptly to your infant and small child when they get distressed, they learn to settle more quickly in the long run because they are safe in the knowledge that their needs for emotional comfort will be met.

Letting your child cry themselves to sleep without any intervention from you is just cruel and against nature. When small babies cry it is because they are communicating distress. That distress might be psychological or physiological, but it doesn't really matter which it is except in as much as it needs to be responded to.

'CONTROLLED CRYING' IS BAD FOR YOUR CHILD – AND FOR YOU

I am horrified by the technique of 'controlled crying' that lots of authors and experts put forward as a tool for responding to a waking child and teaching them not to cry out and disturb their parents at night. Controlled crying involves leaving your child to cry for increasingly long periods before offering comfort. When you do offer comfort you offer it only to a point at which your child calms down and then you leave them again. In other words, when a baby is desperately seeking comfort from real distress, their parent deliberately withholds it. Controlled crying is a behavioural technique that relies on the principle that, if babies and children are left to cry themselves to sleep, they will learn that they get no attention for crying and so ultimately they stop crying.

What babies are actually learning from the technique of controlled crying is that there is no point in crying when they are distressed as they will not be comforted. They are being taught to give up seeking comfort in times of distress as it will not be responded to. Parents who practise controlled crying are knowingly and intentionally abandoning their child at the height of their emotional distress. I find this to be shocking. The process of controlled crying is emotionally traumatizing for babies and for parents. As a result many parents who try it can't fully implement it because they are too distressed themselves listening to their baby cry. Even if the technique always successfully leads to children falling asleep without parental involvement, it is, I think, impossible to argue that this end justifies the cruelty of the means. Controlled crying is emotionally and psychologically bad for children.

> Infants and small children are more likely to develop and maintain secure attachments when their distress is responded to promptly, consistently and appropriately

HELPING THE CHILD WHO FINDS IT HARD TO FALL ASLEEP

If your child either struggles to go to sleep or wakes up during the night, then my strategy for responding is to spend the time with them to help them to fall asleep.

The most important thing you are offering your child is your physical presence. Hand-holding, lullabies, head-stroking and so on are all bonuses. Your child may well become dependent on you or the head-strokes to feel comfortable enough to sleep, but that is not a bad thing, and over time you can slowly wean them off their dependence.

Let's take an example of a three-year-old who likes to hold your hand while falling asleep. Initially, you let them hold your hand and then you might suggest that they hold just one finger. Do this for a few days and then suggest that you will leave your hand on their hand. After some more days you put your hand beside your child and then after that you remain sitting beside them but with your hand in your lap. Slowly, over a series of days, you withdraw more and more, moving the chair further from the bed until you reach a point that you are near the door. From there you spend some time being outside and checking regularly and then again over time you increase the time between checks.

What babies are actually learning from the technique of controlled crying is that there is no point in crying when they are distressed as they will not be comforted

What this lets your child know is that you can still be relied upon to be there, and so their anxiety at being separated has time to settle at each stage before you move to the next one. It may seem like a long and laborious process, but actually you will probably find that, if you are using a pleasant bedtime routine in advance, they are falling asleep quite quickly. Following a process like this is preferable to having them scream and demand your attention, which you give reluctantly and with increasing frustration until eventually they sleep due to exhaustion.

With other children you may find that they don't need or want you to stay with them but in order to lessen their anxiety they like to know that you will be regularly checking on them. You may like to set up a plan with your child that you will come in to check on them (maybe giving another quick kiss or a head-stroke) every five to ten minutes until they are asleep. Once

Controlled crying is emotionally and psychologically bad for children

children realize that you will definitely be coming in to them regularly, it reduces their need to call for you.

If you are not staying with your child as they fall asleep, you may have a child who keeps coming down the stairs to you. If this is the case, then you need to be ready to stay calm and focused and continually return them to bed. Be firm but gentle in the process. As you carry them back to bed, give one clear message that 'this is sleeping time and you need to be in your bed'. Once they are in bed give them a quick kiss and say 'Night, night,' then leave swiftly. Don't be tempted to hang around waiting to see if they come out again. They will know you are there, and you can be sure that they will come out to you. A child coming out of bed like this is seeking attention and so they need the message that this kind of behaviour won't get them the attention they want. Setting up the regular checking visits may also help your child to know that they don't need to come out of bed for your attention and won't be forgotten about.

You may like to set up a plan with your child that you will come in to check on them (maybe giving another quick kiss or head-stroke) every five to ten minutes until they are asleep

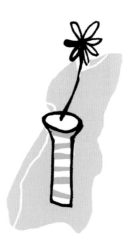

DEALING WITH NIGHTMARES

As with so many childhood experiences you can always be reassured that your child is not the only one who experiences nightmares. In fact, nightmares are common enough and generally start from about the age of two and reach their peak between the ages of three and six years. For whatever reason most nightmares seem to occur in the early hours of the morning (just to make it most disruptive for parents!). The frequency of nightmares varies from child to child. Some children have a frightening dream once or twice a year, and others have them much more regularly. About a quarter of children have at least one nightmare a week.

It is not fully understood why children, or adults for that matter, have nightmares. On the same basis that regular dreams are thought to be a processing of experiences to date it is quite possible that nightmares are a child's attempts to understand, process and resolve frightening, distressing or anxiety-provoking events or experiences.

Once children realize that you will definitely be coming in to them regularly, it reduces their need to call for you

In the aftermath of a trauma, for example, the incidence of nightmares can increase significantly for up to six months or longer. Sometimes it may be that children are simply processing the normal stresses and strains of growing up. Occasionally, fever brings up nightmares, and they are also sometimes found more in children with very active imaginations.

If you are faced with a child's nightmare, then do make sure to respond. Cuddle and reassure them. You need to remember that their feelings are genuine, and ignoring them is not going to make things better and indeed will just further distress them. If you decide that your child is just making up the nightmare to get your sympathy and attention you could end up getting angry, and this also just inflames the distress for your child.

It may take some time for them to settle, and so be prepared to hang in there. If you don't mind having an extra body in your bed, then do take them there, as it will definitely encourage a sense of safety, and your child will settle back to sleep sooner. If they come into your bed and sleep 'safely', they may associate their bed with the nightmare and refuse to use it at all. If you think this will be a problem for you, then whatever bed they are in at the time of the dream you need to encourage them to stay in. Having said that, even if they do come into your bed and then they refuse to use their own bed, it will only be a temporary thing, and they will go back to there eventually.

Depending on their age, they may want to talk to you about the nightmare. Typical themes involve being chased by a frightening person or animal. If your child does talk to you about it, then you could try to create a happy, funny or safe ending to the dream such as the chaser falling into a hole or having a big cage fall down and entrap them or the child being chased managing to outrun the chaser and getting home safely.

SOME SOURCES OF NIGHTMARES

There are other ways of reducing the frequency of nightmares or their impact. You do need to talk to your child, though, and let them know that everyone has dreams and nightmares, and that it is impossible to guarantee that they will go away. By reducing the amount of TV that they are exposed to, especially violent or scary shows, you might help to reduce the frequency of nightmares. I know most parents of pre-schoolers insist they only let their children watch cartoons, but even cartoons contain violence and scary scenes.

Things in your child's daily routine may be troubling or upsetting them, and this could lead to more nightmares

Also, despite protestations to the contrary, most pre-schoolers get exposed to other TV including, for example, the soaps that Mammy or Daddy might watch and the advertising in between. If they have older brothers or sisters, then monitoring their TV exposure is even harder.

Your child, too, may not distinguish accurately between fantasy and reality in what they watch. Do you remember the story I told of how a mum showed me the scar on her

If your child does talk to you about it, then you could try to create a happy, funny or safe ending to the dream such as the chaser falling into a hole or having a big cage fall down and entrap them or the child being chased managing to outrun the chaser and getting home safely

four-year-old son's tummy from where he had injured himself as he jumped from the gatepost, landing on the gate, as he leaped like Spider-Man after casting a web? So even if they are only watching cartoons they may not realize that the things that happen to the characters are only make-believe.

Other things in your child's daily routine may be troubling or upsetting them, and this could lead to more nightmares. So have a think about what is going on in your child's life. Starting school or pre-school may be anxiety-provoking. Maybe there have been other events like marital separation, the death of a relative or moving house. All of these events could be on your child's mind, and then the uncertainty, worry or upset may be expressed in their dreams. This is particularly the case if they do not have the capacity to express it in words because of their age.

KEY POINTS TO REMEMBER

> Circadian rhythms, based on brightness and darkness, are the strongest cues for your child to be awake or asleep.

> By keeping the room dark and dimming the lights during the evening you can lull your child into a sense of sleepiness.

> Sleep, too, follows a regular rhythm and is a process of moving from wakefulness into increasing depth of sleep (non-REM sleep) and then back to near wakefulness (REM sleep).

> Most infants have no rhythm to their sleep for the first four to six months or so.

> Toddlers need twelve to fourteen hours' sleep a day, most of which will happen at night.

> Most children will come awake at night; some can just settle themselves back to sleep (self-soothers), and others need help to do so (signallers).

> Resistance to going to bed is common amongst toddlers and pre-schoolers due sometimes to separation anxiety and sometimes to a developing independence.

> Creating predictable patterns to the day including a bedtime routine gives security to your child and may help to reduce that separation anxiety.

> Avoid TV in bedrooms; it is a stimulant not a relaxant.

> The same goes for some foods like chocolate or cola; in general, sugary drinks are best avoided at night-time.

> A calm bedtime routine also gives messages to your child that sleeping time is approaching and prepares them to settle.

- Bedtime routines should include opportunities for intimacy and warmth, increasing your child's sense of receiving attention such that they will have less need to come looking for that attention after lights out.

- It is OK for children to need your help to fall asleep, and if your child struggles to settle alone or calls out when he wakes, then stay with him until he sleeps – you are helping to develop a secure attachment with your child.

- In contrast, controlled crying, where you leave your child to cry for increasing amounts of time before offering comfort, is emotionally abusive.

- Over time you can wean children off their dependency on you and develop independence at night-times.

- This weaning is helped if your child can rely on you and has security in their relationship with you.

7

MANAGING TOILET-TRAINING

THE ART AND SCIENCE OF SQUIRTING AND SQUATTING

Toilet-training remains one of the more unglamorous tasks for parents. Despite this, it is a very significant stage of development for a child, and getting it right gives your child an important sense of control. Becoming aware of and in control of your bowel and bladder seems to us adults (who are so practised in the art) to be one of those instinctual and natural things that we inherently 'know' how to do. And it is a very instinctual and natural stage for children to achieve but it involves some complex learning. That means we adults have to give the process time and avoid rushing it or getting frustrated in the middle of it and giving our children mixed messages about their wees and poos.

Importantly, too, we need to remember that only our toddlers can let their wees and poos come out, and that means ultimately they have the power to decide when and where it happens. Most toddlers, when feeling pressure, will become tense, and tense toddlers can stay tightly clamped shut! Too much pressure from parents can lead to some pretty significant defiance. Therefore, the art of toilet-training is knowing when to encourage and knowing when to simply wait.

THIS CHAPTER LOOKS AT ...

How to know when to begin the process

Preparations for toilet-training

From preparation to performance – encouraging nature to take her course

Dealing with inevitable accidents

Moving into the night-times

Dealing with persistent bed-wetting

HOW TO KNOW WHEN TO BEGIN

You can start to train your child from as young as eighteen months, but all of the research shows that when you start younger the process takes longer. It is almost as if the point at which a child learns to use the toilet is pre-set, and, if you start too soon, it just takes longer to reach that point.

There are some things that we can introduce to our children when they are not ready, and they cope fine. Toilet-training is not one of them. If you begin the process too early, then you run the risk of distressing your child and yourself. If you start when they are very young and they struggle to get the concept, it is quite likely to be a frustrating experience for you and your child. Learning to master control of your bowel and bladder are important developmental steps for every child. But the feeling of failure if mastery

> Don't be misled by stuff that you might read or hear about most children being toilet-trained when they are two years of age. As with any developmental task there is a wide range of 'normal'

is not achieved can be acute. Nobody likes to feel like they are failing, and so it can be very disheartening if the process seems to take a long time. This is even more the case if your parents are very invested in you achieving this control.

Don't be misled by stuff that you might read or hear about most children being toilet-trained when they are two years of age. As with any developmental task there is a wide range of 'normal', and it is quite common for children to train anywhere between the ages of two and four years. A small few children will be before that and some may be after that.

It is a good idea, then, to give your child the best possible chance of success by ensuring that they are developmentally ready and showing some interest in the process themselves. This means that the process is more likely to be child-centred. In other words, your child will lead the process, and you will guide it. They will show signs of when they want to be trained, and you will show them how to do it.

Waiting until your child is ready means, however, that you may have to put some of your own needs second. It may suit you, for example, to have your child fully trained before they go to pre-school, and in fact many pre-schools insist on children being trained before they start. Unfortunately, it may not suit your child. You may want them to be trained before you go away on a long break or holiday, but your child may not be ready.

Even if you have external pressures bearing on your decision to train your child, I would still encourage you to wait until your child shows the developmental readiness and the interest. Those developmental indicators of readiness are:

☆ **That they can walk and sit down**. It may seem obvious, but in today's culture the rush to get children toilet-trained is staggering. If your child can't independently stand up, walk around and sit down, they are never going to manage the physical requirements of getting to the potty or toilet.

You may want them trained before you go away on a long break or holiday, but your child may not be ready

☆ **That they can pull their pants up and down**. This is another physical motor skill that your child needs. The possibility of accidents is greatly increased if nimble fingers are not nimble enough to grasp and pull. Also, if your child is relying on you to pull up or down their pants, then they are not going to be independent.

☆ **That they can follow simple instructions**. A simple instruction is one that has just one step in it, like 'pick up your toy' or 'bring me the paper'. This shows that their receptive language skills are good enough to be able to understand the instructions and guidance that you will have to give about using the potty or toilet.

★ **That they have words for stool and urine.** In our house we use the terms 'poos' and 'wees', but it varies from family to family. If your child goes to a crèche or pre-school, then it is worth finding out what words they use as, when the time comes for toilet-training, you will need their assistance to support your efforts, and your child's, while they are in the crèche.

★ **That they have dry periods of three to four hours.** You will be able to tell from their nappy whether they are achieving this. For example, when you change their nappy before bed or if you are changing before swimming, you may notice that the nappy is dry. Over the next while you can monitor this to see if there are indeed long dry periods, meaning that your child's bladder has matured enough to contain their wee.

Aside from their developmental progress there are other signs that your toddler can give you that she might be interested and ready to toilet-train. These include:

★ **They have regular bowel movements.** You may notice that your child does their poo at fairly predictable times of the day. In fact, the same can be said for lots of us! Most children will do a poo at least once a day, sometimes more. If you begin to pay attention to their habits you will probably notice that the poo comes within an hour of eating something. This is handy information to remember, as it can help you later when you actually start the process – it means you can encourage toileting at times when you know the chances of success are greater. My own son, for example, who is two (and not yet toilet-trained), will usually poo within an hour of his breakfast in the morning.

★ **It is obvious when they are going to the toilet.** Once your child is getting closer to the age of training, you will notice that their pooing in particular becomes more obvious. They may squat to go, or you will hear them grunting, or they may tell you just before or after. It is especially helpful if they can recognize the physical sensations of needing to go to the toilet and tell you before. Being in tune with their body in this way is a real bonus for starting to toilet-train, as it means that they will probably find it much quicker to get success at using the potty or toilet and they will have fewer accidents. The older a child is, the more likely they are to recognize the physical signs in their own body of being ready to go.

They indicate discomfort after dirtying their nappy. This sign often is associated with the previous indicator; if your child comes to tell you that they have done a poo and wants their nappy changed. This feeling of discomfort can be a good motivator for your child once you begin the process, as you can encourage them to use the potty or toilet to avoid having to go around with a pooey bum.

They show an interest in others' toileting. Weeing and pooing are very interesting things for toddlers, and once your toddler begins to show a definite interest in following you or their siblings into the bathroom to watch, it is another good sign that they may be ready to learn to use the bathroom themselves. Much better to encourage your toddler's interest rather than discourage it – even if you suffer some mild performance anxiety about weeing in front of them!

They show an interest in independence. This can be a general interest in becoming more independent. I remember hearing the phrase 'I'll do it my own self' used in many different situations in our house and by each of the children as they moved through toddlerhood. Everything from fastening the safety harness on the car seat to pouring water from the jug had to be attempted as part of their move to independence.

As with all things in parenting you have to use your own judgement about how far along on the readiness scale your child is. Not all of the things I have listed need to have been achieved or demonstrated. If they have and are, though, then you can be surer that the process of training will be easier and quicker. Once you feel that your child is ready, there are a few things you can do to prepare the way for training to begin.

PREPARATIONS FOR TOILET-TRAINING

When you think about toilet-training your child, you need to be thinking in the slightly longer term rather than the short term. The process of training can take several months, even though there are websites that proclaim the task can be achieved in three days! Be realistic in your expectations so that you don't end up frustrated and giving negative messages to your child when it doesn't go as quickly or as smoothly as the guides will tell you.

One of the most important things to remember is that this is a big developmental step for your child, and so you want to allow it to happen in as stress-free an environment as possible. This means that you don't want toilet-training to be competing with things like moving house, changing child-minder or crèche, you changing job, or a new baby arriving into the family. Toddlers are lovers of routine, and if big events are going to disrupt that routine, then they will also disrupt your toddler. If you are trying to toilet-train in the midst of uncertainty and change, then you can be sure it will be more stressful and probably less successful for you and your toddler. Using the toilet is as much about habit and routine as any other part of your child's day, and you need to feel like you have the space to be incorporating just this one new habit.

This is a big developmental step for your child

FINDING THE PERFECT POTTY AND THE PERFECT PANTS

As part of your preparations you need to get a few tools of the trade ready. Most obviously, you need a potty. You might like to bring your toddler with you to purchase the potty; that way at least you stand a better chance of getting one that he or she will like. Some people prefer to get inserts for the toilet seat rather than a potty. This is OK so long as you ensure that the insert fits snugly on to the seat and doesn't slip as your child manoeuvres themselves on to it. You will also need a step or stool (we call it a 'stepper' in our house; it is made of lightweight plastic and is easy and manageable for our two-year-old to lift) to help them climb to the height of the seat on their own. They will also need this step to rest their feet on to provide a bit of resistance while they push (during their poo) and also to stabilize them so that they don't feel like they will fall off. The same stepper is likely to be of help to get them up to the sink to wash their hands afterwards too.

Getting the right potty or seat insert is important, as many toddlers fear falling into the toilet

Getting the right potty or seat insert is important, as many toddlers fear falling into the toilet. Unsurprisingly, that anxiety is highly likely to block their progress in using the toilet. Potties have the added advantages of being portable and so can be used in any room in the house. A potty can be claimed as your toddler's very own, including perhaps being festooned with stickers or their name to personalize it. Against that, they are an intermediate step to using the toilet, and so getting comfortable with a regular toilet still has to be achieved at some stage down the line.

Underwear is another vital ingredient in the preparation. The thrill of picking out your first pairs of underwear is underestimated by us grown-ups but can be a big and reinforcing deal for a toddler. Having underwear emblazoned with their favourite superhero or toy can be a big motivator to get out of nappies and into the grown-up world.

The thrill of picking out your first pairs of underwear is underestimated by us grown-ups

Some people espouse the value of training pants, or pull-ups, as an intermediate stage between nappies and underpants or knickers. I am not a fan of these, as they are more likely to confuse a child who doesn't get any sensation of wetness when they wee and so may not have even realized that they have done a wee.

However, if you are going the route of pants rather than pull-ups, you do need to be prepared for accidents. While it might be a quicker and more definitive process to wear pants, you may get too stressed by the pools of wee soaking into the carpet or spreading over the wood or tiles. There is no point in stressing yourself unduly, as your stress will definitely transfer to your child and potentially disrupt the whole process. Go with your gut and whatever you think you can handle. If you can manage the inevitable accidents, then pants from the outset are your best bet. Besides, moving up to big boy or girl pants is an exciting time.

If your child is in full- or part-time childcare, then you need to talk to their minder about your decision to start toilet-training and especially this issue of moving into underwear and out of nappies. You can be sure that your childcare provider will have an opinion on what will and won't work when your child is with them. Obviously, if your child is at home being minded, you can probably dictate a little more. If your child goes out to be minded, then you may have to go along with the practice of your minder.

> **If you can manage the inevitable accidents, then pants from the outset are your best bet**

THE WORLD IS FULL OF TOILET-TRAINING EXPERTS

Having said all that, you will probably find that everyone you meet will be an expert on toilet-training, and those who have had children will have their guaranteed method that 'worked like a dream' to nip those nappies in the bud within days. Take it with a pinch of salt. Opinions have changed over the years. Thirty or forty years ago, for example, there was no child-centredness preached, and so training occurred at a set point, often as early as possible. So don't feel pressured by in-laws or your parents to rush into toilet-training. You may have to agree to disagree about the best time to start and even how to go about the process. Be confident in yourself and, unless they are minding your child for more of the time than you are, stick to your guns about how you want to achieve toileting for your child.

> **Don't feel pressured by in-laws or your parents to rush into toilet-training**

The only other thing you might like to buy is a child-focused story book about toileting to read to them. This might provide the inspiration your son or daughter needs to launch them into the process.

GETTING YOUR CHILD POTTY-FRIENDLY

Once you have a potty or seat insert, you can encourage your child to sit on it once a day, with their nappy and clothes on. I suggest keeping clothes on at first simply because the plastic can feel cold and hard, and you don't want their first experience of sitting on the potty to be negative. It is not about sitting for any particular length of time either; it is simply about increasing familiarity by practising. If your child seems happy to sit, then chat away for a few minutes or read them a story or sing them a song. What you are trying to do is to associate pleasant experiences with sitting on the potty. If they are uncomfortable for any reason and don't want to sit, then don't force them. Take it as a sign that they are not ready and come back to it in a few weeks. If they do get used to sitting, then, after about a week of this, you can do the same thing but with no nappy on.

At this stage you are still preparing the ground, so don't go expecting them to perform. Your only goal is to get your child used to including the potty in their normal daily routine. Do take the opportunity to talk about the intended purpose of the potty at this stage and, if you like, you can get their favourite teddy or dolly to role-model the sitting behaviour. You

You may even like to get or make a little potty for teddy so that your child and teddy can sit side by side

may even like to get or make a little potty for teddy so that your child and teddy can sit side by side. If they do sit side by side you may notice that your child will make believe that teddy is weeing or pooing, and this could prove inspirational for your child with their wees and poos. Let them sit each day with no pants on, in exactly the same way, for a further week, and by that stage you and they are probably ready to move on to the real thing.

FROM PREPARATION TO PERFORMANCE – ENCOURAGING NATURE TO TAKE HER COURSE

Once you and your offspring are clear about the purpose of the potty, and they are comfortable sitting on it, you need simply to give the message that the time has come to start using it for its intended purpose. Then you wait.

It seems like it should be more complex, but actually it isn't. You wait for the first time that your child does a wee or a poo and then you celebrate like you just won the lottery. This is a big deal, and your child needs to know that you think so too. Reward their first time with something significant like an extra bedtime story or some extra one-to-one playtime. After that first time, however, you can tone down the praise and acknowledgement. Do still recognize both the attempts and the successes but do it in a more laid-back and matter-of-fact way. If you keep making too big a deal of every potty

If you keep making too big a deal of every potty trip, you could just make them nervous or self-conscious, as the glare of the spotlight might be just too much

trip, you could just make them nervous or self-conscious, as the glare of the spotlight might be just too much.

Also, too much encouragement and praise can leave a child feeling guilty if they have an accident. If too much of a focus has been put on the potty and successful use of it, they can feel like they are letting you down if they are not successful. I'll talk about dealing with accidents in more detail below. For the time being, just think of modestly praising and avoiding being over the top.

Of course, if you are too modest and understated, then you may struggle to keep their enthusiasm high. You need to strike a balance between keeping it real and keeping it exciting. For example, you will be remembering to be catching the benefit of their natural digestion and always bringing them to the potty after meals, but trying to keep the experience fun and engaging. You will also be encouraging them to take a trip to the toilet or potty at other regular intervals. At the start this will be a novelty for your child, but the gloss can be worn away quickly. To keep your own mood positive you can think about the fact that you are on a path to no more nappies. Once you are thinking positively, you will find it easier to keep distracting your child with songs, stories or games to help pass the time while waiting for nature to kick in.

WHAT TO DO WHEN YOUR CHILD IS NO LONGER POTTY ABOUT THE POTTY

If, after you have become established in training, the initial excitement does wear off, you may find that your toddler's interest wanes. They may be less motivated to try and they may not see a great point in investing in using the potty or toilet. As well as the verbal praise you may then like to introduce something like a star chart or sticker chart to add to the reinforcement of successful use of the potty. I have explained star charts in more detail in chapter 5, but, briefly, they are a way of visually recording the successes. Every time a wee or a poo goes into the toilet, you give your child a sticker or star to add to their chart.

You may then like to introduce something like a star chart

For small children just the star itself can be reinforcing and rewarding. For other children you may want to have the build-up of stars as a journey to a bigger goal. For example, after five stars are collected, your child becomes eligible for a treat of some kind, like more of your attention.

Other ideas, to make toilet time fun, include putting some favourite books or comics into the bathroom so that your child can amuse themselves while they wait. Either they can look at them themselves or you have a ready-stocked pile to read from. Another tip that I only recently heard about and haven't yet tried is to drip some blue food colourant into the toilet bowl, and then your child will be amazed at how their wee will turn the water from blue to green. Other people decide, if they are using a potty, that they will allow the potty to be in the child's favourite room where they spend most of their time so that the minimum of disturbance needs to

Maybe put some favourite books or comics into the bathroom

occur if the urge to wee comes. In other words, if your daughter loves her bedroom, then let her wee there, surrounded by her toys and things to help her stay distracted if a wait is involved.

Another tip to speed up the process is to let your child go around with nothing on their bottom half. A little bit of nakedness will help your toddler figure out sooner when they need to go. If you have a potty, then this may be the time to have it in the room with them. By being naked from the waist down they are essentially ready to go, and so it is easier to encourage them to sit at regular intervals, without the palaver of getting out of and then back into their underwear and trousers. Also, when you spot the signs that a wee or poo may be coming

Let your child go around with nothing on their bottom half. Toddlers touching their genitals are very normal

(like clutching themselves or jumping up and down, or suddenly squatting, or getting a pained look on their face), you can remind them quickly that these cues mean it is probably potty time and they are already ready. The downside is the potential for many and regular accidents along the way. Like using pants instead of pull-ups, naked bums are only to be recommended if you can sustain the patience required to clean up the leakages that will inevitably occur.

YOUNG CHILDREN AND THEIR GENITALS

Another possible problem for some parents is that once there is no nappy in the way, your child quickly realizes that there is the potential for unlimited access to their genitals. For some children this is no big deal, and they are nonplussed about exploring their bits. For others the exploration and the associated pleasure of the touch is very rewarding and they can quickly get in the habit of touching themselves a lot.

Toddlers touching their genitals are very normal. Even what appears like excessive touching happens for lots of children. The message you give to your child at this point is really quite important. You need to let them know that there is nothing wrong with touching themselves, and that their genitals are as healthy and natural a part of themselves as their toes and fingers. At the same time, they need to realize that there is a time and place for touching their bits. That time and place are when other people aren't around and they have some

> While we are on the topic of penises and vaginas, do use those terms with your child

privacy. So don't get cross and don't punish your child for the touch. Just guide their hand away and if you can, distract them, while telling them that touching their penis or vagina is OK, but not in public.

While we are on the topic of penises and vaginas, do use those terms with your child. Interchanging them with other colloquialisms such as 'willie', 'pee-pee', 'bum' and so on is OK, but it is good for your child to know the correct terminology, if for no other reason than that it will reduce their embarrassment when they are faced with the real names later on. It is quite a personal thing and often reflects our own values whether we use real names or slang names. Sometimes it is our own discomfort with the names for our bits that prevents us from teaching our children.

READY, AIM ... SPRAY

Some people get hung up on the issue of boys sitting or standing at the start of toilet-training. In reality it isn't a particularly big deal whether they stand or sit. Since wees will often come at the same time as a poo, it probably makes more sense to initially encourage your son to sit rather than stand. However, standing has the benefit of being very reinforcing, as the whole operation is visible to view, wees splattering into a potty or toilet bowl sound great, and your son can handle his own equipment in the process. It doesn't really get better for small boys!

Boys who have been watching their dads or big brothers may be intent on standing anyway. Doing things 'just like my daddy' is hard and potentially counter-productive to argue against. If you find that your son insists on standing, you'll notice that they may be reluctant to sit at all, and therefore beginning to poo in the potty gets delayed. Don't worry – their insistence on standing is usually a temporary affair and sooner or later they will realize that daddy sits sometimes, and that they must sit sometimes too.

Unfortunately, most learner toileters have terrible aim, and the wee is as likely to go all around the bowl as into it. If it is the case that your boy insists on standing, there are a few things you can do to improve his aim.

> You can drop some breakfast cereal pieces into the bowl and encourage your son to try to sink them. This works for dads and older sons too!

Firstly try getting him to stand on the step or stool and to use the toilet. Toilet bowls are significantly larger than potties and so the target is bigger. Then you can drop some breakfast cereal pieces into the bowl and encourage your son to try to sink them. This works for dads and older sons too! Alternatively, you can get him to cut out some paper shapes and drop them into the bowl for target practice. Both of these things will increase the interest levels of your son in weeing into the toilet rather than anywhere else. There is also the food dye to try.

Before I move on to dealing with accidents, and while I am thinking about wee spraying everywhere, it is a good idea to promote hand-washing after using the potty or toilet from day one. If you associate the two from the start it will form a habit of a lifetime. If you miss out on the opportunity you may find that you have to work harder to link them later. Being a good role-model is a great start. There is no point in promoting a notion based on what you say but not what you do. So make sure, if your son or daughter is watching you use the bathroom, that they get to see the final step of hands being washed.

When it comes to their turn to use the potty, you can guide them to the sink afterwards and, using a stool or step, let them up high enough to be able to reach the soap and the taps. Help them with the washing. To increase their motivation to use the sink you might also want to designate a specially coloured or shaped bar of soap

The key to successfully dealing with accidents is to remain calm

to use or a special towel for them to dry their hands in only after using the potty. Star or sticker charts will also work well to reinforce hand-washing; just make sure it is a separate chart from the potty-use one. You don't want to be in the position of not being able to give a star for a successful wee because they then forgot to wash their hands.

DEALING WITH ACCIDENTS

Accidents are bound to happen. Children will get it wrong and make mistakes when it comes to toileting. Unlike in lots of other situations they sometimes seem slow to learn from their mistakes. That means that they can miss making it to the toilet or potty on lots of occasions. The key to successfully dealing with accidents is to remain calm.

If the accidents are happening more frequently than the successes, then it may be that your child is not quite ready

The one guaranteed fact is that nothing will disrupt toilet-training faster than making your child feel bad for having an accident. You are well aware at this stage that I encourage you to stay in charge of your feelings anyway in dealing with your child, but it is especially crucial when it comes to wees or poos on the floor, in pants or on the sofa. Getting criticized or given out to will just increase your child's anxiety about their ability to achieve the stage of using the toilet and it may increase their resistance to even trying.

You can take it for granted that your child didn't mean to wet themselves or the floor. All small children can have toileting accidents. They get engrossed in play and they don't pay attention to the signals from their body in enough time. Even children who may seem well established in their trips to the potty can have an accident. If you scold or give out, then the feeling of failure and of disappointing you can easily lead your child to give up, and then you end up back having to deal with those nappies!

I never realized how long car journeys could be extended by due to unscheduled wee stops until I had children

Whenever you come across an accident, respond as simply and as matter-of-factly as you can. Comment on what you see in a non-judgemental way, for example: 'The wee is on the floor, it didn't make it into the potty. Next time you can get the wee into the potty.' Remember from the chapter on communication that the tone of your voice and the look on your face are probably telling your child more than your words are so make sure that they reflect the same calm acceptance that your words give off.

Depending on the point at which you have discovered the accident (after the event or in mid-flow), you may want to bring them to the potty to finish off, saying, 'Some wee went in your pants, now you can get the rest of it in the potty.' If it is clearly a done deal when you arrive, with a nice big pool spreading slowly across the floor, then don't make a fuss or force them to go to the bathroom to 'finish off'. Do bring them to change but don't keep referencing the mess.

As in all things, practice will improve their performance, and so, even if there are accidents, it is important to keep trying. If the accidents are happening more frequently than the successes, then it may be that your child is not quite ready. Think back to the readiness guide I gave earlier. If, in retrospect, you think that maybe your child isn't ready, then you can just tell them that you are going to stick with nappies again for a while because their body isn't quite ready and that you will be trying again when they are a little older.

If your toddler manages to tell you they need to go, then do respond quickly. Most children of this age don't get a lot of warning from their bodies and so, if they have to go, then they have to go. Don't be tempted to chop that last carrot, or finish the last few mouthfuls of food on your plate, before you assist. Time is of the essence! I never realized how long car journeys could be extended by due to unscheduled wee stops until I had children. If someone had invented a car seat with integrated potty I'd have bought it. As you head for the potty or toilet, you can give a few words of praise for managing to hold on en route. This might also then give your child a sense of accomplishment that they have a little bit of control over their bladder.

If your toddler manages to tell you they need to go, then do respond quickly. Most children of this age don't get a lot of warning from their bodies and so, if they have to go, then they have to go ... Time is of the essence!

MOVING INTO THE NIGHT-TIMES

There are a few important factors to consider before moving into training at night. Mind you, even that concept of training at night is misleading. In fact, staying dry through the night is much more of a developmental thing over which you have little control.

When you first start toilet-training during the day, you will probably keep your child in nappies at night. Wait until your child goes through the day without accidents and is securely toilet-trained. When you reach this point then you can start checking your child's nappy after naps or in the morning. Don't forget that you could be three to six months into the process (or longer); as with everything to do with toileting, don't be in a hurry. Your child will guide you.

So after the daytime training has kicked in, you may notice that your child wakes up in the morning with a dry nappy. This is the best indicator that your child is ready to sleep all night without a nappy. Don't be tempted to put them into pull-ups as an intermediate step. If you think they can be dry, then go straight from nappies to pyjamas. You might want to invest in a waterproof breathable undersheet to protect the mattress, as accidents do indeed happen.

Staying dry at night is a bit more difficult for children to control, as it depends on how deeply they sleep

Staying dry at night is a bit more difficult for children to control, as it depends on how deeply they sleep. If your daughter sleeps deeply, she may not get the messages from her bladder that it needs to be emptied. Some children develop the capacity to hold wee, and so, despite not waking, they stay dry. Other children need to be alerted by the 'I'm bursting to go' feeling that they will get in the night but may not know how, or may not be able, to respond to it.

So even if you are not sure how it will go, it is worth giving the nights a try and seeing how your child does, especially if they are asking to sleep without nappies. If you find that the majority of nights end up wet, then, as with the daytimes, it is a sign that they are not ready. As when dealing with the persistent daytime accidents, you give a really non-judgemental message about your child's body not being ready and say that you'll try again in a while when he or she is bigger.

Don't be put off if this all seems to be taking an age. Almost half of all children will wet the bed up to the age of three. Night-time accidents are very normal up to the age of seven with approximately one in ten children still wetting at night. There does seem to be a strong family component to bed-wetting also. Research studies show that about three-quarters of children whose parents both wet the bed as youngsters will do the same. Not quite half of children with one bed-wetting parent will follow suit, and only about an eighth of children where neither parent had any trouble staying dry will wet the bed. So maybe you can blame it on the genes. This is cold comfort, of course, if yours is one of those children who do wet the bed, and you end up with the additional laundry and the disruption to your sleep. There are things you can try to do to promote night-time dryness, and I'll look at that in the next section.

Stumbling and sleepy is never the best way to greet a damp bed and a distressed child

DEALING WITH PERSISTENT BED-WETTING

Some children who wet the bed can sleep through it and don't even get disturbed by their wet sheets and duvets. While this leads to a very strong and sustained smell of ammonia, it does have the benefit of not disturbing anyone else's sleep. I say this because our children never managed to sleep on. Inevitably, within seconds of the accident, we'd hear the cries of anguish. In the recent past we've got into the habit of my wife responding to the baby (well, toddler) and me responding to the older two if they wake at night. It has become so well established in our house that, at night, I don't even hear our youngest cry sometimes, and my wife rarely hears the older ones. So when the cries come it is usually me who goes in. Stumbling and sleepy is never the best way to greet a damp bed and a distressed child. I'll own up to the fact that grumpiness has often meant that I haven't responded as ideally as I should.

Of course, what I should do is give the same non-judgemental message as ever – that accidents happen, and let's just sort the bed out. But when you are faced with having to find clean pyjamas, sheets and/or duvet as well as comforting and cleaning a weeping four-year-old, it is a bit trying. The real world is never as ideal as the guides written by people like me make out.

Anyway, this is all simply to justify that it is worth investing in trying to resolve the problem, and, as in the daytimes, you can give nature a helping hand.

Do restrict drinks in the evenings if your child persistently wets the bed. Liquid will, inevitably, be digested and most of it ends up as wee. If it has gone in it must come out. In the same way always insist on a final wee before bed. This then means that you are likely to be giving your child the best chance of having space to contain whatever will be produced.

I think it is OK to lift a child to the toilet before you go to bed yourself. Some people believe that you set up bad habits, and that your child relies on being lifted and so never learns to wake themselves or to hold on to whatever is there. I'm not so sure that the evidence is there to back this up. Lifting a child does often work, even though you do end up doing it for a while before it no longer becomes necessary. I am always amazed that, if necessary, I can get my daughter out of her bed, guide her walking into the bathroom, help her sit on the toilet, whisper in her ear that she is on the toilet and now is the time for the wees to come, wait for a few seconds for the gush to happen, help her pull up her pyjama bottoms and guide her back to bed all without her ever fully waking up. That two-minute routine has saved me many nights of stumbling around at 1 a.m. trying to make enough noise that my wife will wake up to help me change the bed.

> **Lifting a child does often work, even though you do end up doing it for a while before it no longer becomes necessary.**

If your bed-wetting child is a little bit older, then you might also like to try a 'pad and bell' system. These systems basically involve a little area of plastic-type material, the pad, which is sensitive to water. You put the pad under your child's sheet. The pad is connected to a little bell or buzzer, and as soon as wetness hits the pad, it sends a signal that sounds the bell, and this wakes your child, who then stumbles to the bathroom to finish the wee. The theory is that at the first release of wee your child gets woken up and so over time becomes more alert to the starting sensation of wee coming and so will wake themselves. These 'pad and bell' systems are available, along with some guidance, from your local health centre.

Sometimes only patience and positive thinking are required, and you will find that your son or daughter will mature in their own good time, and dry nights will come with that maturity.

KEY POINTS TO REMEMBER

➤ **Don't start too early: most children train somewhere between two and four years of age.**

➤ **Rely on signs of readiness such as interest in toileting, interest in independence,** ability to follow instructions, ability to get clothes on and off, regularity of bowel movements and that your child indicates discomfort after dirtying their nappy, to know when to begin.

Prepare for toilet-training by practising sitting on the potty, buying underwear and talking about what will be involved.

Once you begin the process, ensure that you sit your child on the potty at regular times of the day.

Reward success by praising but don't go over the top.

Using a star chart might help to keep motivation high if interest in the process wanes after a few weeks.

Respond to accidents with calmness and never scold.

If accidents occur more than successes, then you may have started too soon, and it could be worth waiting and starting again in a couple of weeks or months.

Once daytime toileting is established (it can take three to six months), you can consider night-times.

Apply the same calm reactions to night-time accidents as you do in the daytime.

Remember that bed-wetting can be genetic and is really common up to three years of age and still is normal up to the age of seven years.

Avoid drinks and encourage doing a wee before bed.

A pad and bell system, for an older child (four to six years), may help your child to learn to recognize the signals, at night, that they need to go to the bathroom.

Be patient.

8

FINDING AN EASY WAY TO EATING

YOU CAN LEAD A CHILD TO WATER, BUT YOU CAN'T MAKE THEM DRINK

The 'problem' of children eating too much or not eating enough exercises the minds of most parents at some stage in their parenting career. In most situations parents really only get worried if their child doesn't eat enough. Because of a genuine fear that their child will not be getting enough nutrition they start on the path of encouraging their child to eat and then move into forcing their child to eat. We don't necessarily physically force-feed our child but we emotionally pressurize them to eat. Our intentions are probably based on a valid premise – that it is important for children to eat, but the practices we engage in end up making our lives and the lives of our children a misery.

HOW PICKINESS DIDN'T DO ME ANY HARM
(THOUGH IT MAY HAVE GIVEN MY PARENTS A FEW HEADACHES)

I need to put some of my own personal cards out on the table here: I was that fussy eater. I was picky, I was choosy and I ate a very limited range of foods. I existed on a diet of cornflakes, toast, lime marmalade, sausages and mashed potatoes with gravy. I imagine I could have easily broken my parents' hearts. Of course, I don't really believe that I did. All the time, as a child, I knew what I wanted to eat and I also knew what I didn't want to eat. I knew when I wanted to eat and I knew when I didn't want to eat. I knew how much I wanted to eat and I knew how much I didn't want to eat. Despite all of my parents' efforts, the basic facts could never be changed, and they could never make me eat something I didn't want to.

> **I existed on a diet of cornflakes, toast, lime marmalade, sausages and mashed potatoes with gravy**

I didn't expand my tastes and become more adventurous until I was sixteen and went away to France for three weeks. I quickly realized that, if I didn't eat the very different range of foods that I was being offered over there, I was going to starve. Of course my brain and body weren't going to let that happen, and so I tried, I tasted and – surprise, surprise – I enjoyed a whole load of new foods. It was quite a revelation to me, and when I returned from France, I continued to experiment and eat much more widely.

All the way through my childhood, despite my restricted diet, I remained fit, healthy and of average weight. I was certainly never sickly or about to fade away. The moral that I always take from my own personal tale is that, as long as there is food made available to children, they will choose to eat and they will determine how much and when they will do it. If children have choices about what food they eat, they will make choices; if they don't have choices, they will eat enough of what's on offer to keep them going.

THERE'S MORE TO FOOD THAN EATING

For some of us, eating 'problems' are a brief issue quickly resolved. For others, they drag on for years and are the cause of significant amounts of stress for you and your child. What we need to remember is that food and eating are more than simple biological and physiological imperatives. Food is intimately bound up with feeling. Those feelings about food might be associated with caring, nurturing, comfort and warmth, or conversely with control, power, deprivation and rejection.

I remained fit, healthy and of average weight

Your own experience of food will have had emotional overtones, and sometimes food remains an emotive issue for us. No wonder, then, that we get so hung up on our children's eating.

Children experience food in just the same way. For example, your child's refusal to eat his dinner is often as much about his determination to show you he is in control as it is about his liking or not of the meal. Food (and our children's food habits) press lots of our emotional buttons, usually for the worst. As with lots of other areas of childcare, we can have unrealistic expectations of our children when it comes to food and how much they eat.

Indeed, when we start to question our own eating habits, we can suddenly realize that actually we are quite different from other people, even though we are normal. The same is true for children. Despite this, we will badger, cajole, plead and insist that our children eat. Listen to yourself at the dinner table tonight.

'Just three more spoonfuls and you're done.'

'Have one bite for Mammy and one bite for Daddy.'

'If you don't finish that, you are not having dessert.'

'Please, darling, just eat a little bit more for me.'

'Look, here is the aeroplane; open wide ...'

'This is delicious. Just try it. Why won't you even try it?'

'If you eat all your chicken, I'll get you a treat from the press.'

'You are not leaving this table until all of that food is gone.'

'Come on, hurry up. It isn't going to taste any better when it is cold.'

'Look at your sister. She has eaten it all. Why won't you?'

It is so easy to construct mealtimes as a battleground in which we and our children are pitched against each other. It doesn't have to be this way. The trouble often is that the eating 'problem' may have been there for as long as you can remember, and the thoughts of changing things can be too overwhelming. But it can be done. You can change your child's eating habits, but it will probably involve changing your own habits too.

We can have unrealistic expectations of our children when it comes to food and how much they eat

NORMAL EATING HABITS

Even as I write this I recognize that it is something of a misnomer. The idea that there is 'a normal eating habit' is a myth. The range of foods, the amount of food and the ways in which children eat vary enormously. When we adults eat, we rarely question if our eating habits are normal. We don't wonder if other people like the same kinds of food or like it served in the same way. Is it more normal to like runny eggs or hard-boiled eggs? Is it more normal to eat a kiwi fruit with the skin on or off? Should I always have a fork in my left hand? If I'm not hungry should I eat anyway because it is dinnertime? Am I odd because I get hungry at 11 a.m. and like a snack? If I haven't finished my sandwich, am I entitled to eat a yogurt anyway?

A normal approach to eating for an adult is to pay attention to the signals from our bodies and to eat when we are hungry and stop when we are full. It is normal to eat a balance of foods but not necessarily the same amount or range every day. It is normal to eat or not eat because you want to and not because you 'should'. If these are normal expectations for adults then they must also be normal expectations for children.

Sometimes we might think that we eat because we want to, but actually there is a strong biological imperative driving us to eat. Our bodies and our minds instinctively know that we need food to survive. We eat because we must live. We eat because we must grow. We eat because we must move. The comforting thing about having a biological imperative is that it affects everybody. Both the tiniest baby and the most troublesome toddler instinctively know that they must eat simply because they are human.

WHY SOME CHILDREN WON'T EAT

If that is the case, you might ask then: why do children choose not to eat? After all, if they instinctively know that they must eat, then surely it would naturally follow that they would eat. The answer for those children who refuse to eat is that somewhere along the way their experiences with food have been negative, their messages about food have become confused, and resistance has built up that is as much about the dynamic of their relationship with you as it is about the food on their plate.

The reality is that, if most children were left completely unhindered and with a range of different foods available to them they would eat – guaranteed. What the children and babies would choose to do is to determine what they eat, how much they eat and when they eat. In other words, like a grazing animal they would eat as hunger came upon them and they would stop eating when they got a message from their stomachs that they were full.

One of the main difficulties that parents face in thinking about and trying to understand their child's eating behaviour is that their own expectations for their child are often way off the mark. Unfortunately in our culture, we have decided the times that children must eat; we determine the amount that they must eat and we usually choose what they will eat. These choices are based on what we believe is right for our children not necessarily what they want or need.

> **Both the tiniest baby and the most troublesome toddler instinctively know that they must eat simply because they are human**

Because we are doing the choosing we often get it wrong. We pick the wrong kind of food, or we offer it too soon – before, developmentally, they can cope – or we expect them to eat more than they need and want. Small babies and small children have no way of telling you what, how much and when they want to eat and so they leave it up to us to guess. Invariably, they complain if we guess wrong.

Unfortunately we misunderstand these complaints. When they turn their head or spit food out, we think that they are being bold, bad, whingey, picky, fussy and oppositional. In the meantime, they are trying to work out why their parent, who is normally very good at understanding them, always gets it so wrong when it comes to food. Why doesn't Mum get it when they try to explain? It's pretty baffling and pretty upsetting for most children.

Once we misunderstand their refusal to eat we begin the process of trying to trick, cajole, plead and ultimately force them to eat. In the meantime, our children are becoming more resistant to what they perceive as bullying and unreasonable behaviour. After all, if they are getting a message from their stomachs that they don't need the food, they can't suddenly override this just because their parents want them to eat. And so a terrible negative and downward spiral of interaction about food begins. Our first task, then, is to judge how much food our children need in order to live, and on that basis we might make better judgements about how much and when to offer food.

HOW MUCH FOOD DO CHILDREN NEED?

In some ways there is no real answer to the question of how much food children need. It's a bit like asking: how long is a piece of string? The amount of food that children need will be determined by their size, by their level of growth and by their level of activity. A bigger child will need more food than a smaller child. A child who is busy and active will burn up more energy than a child who is not busy. A child who is in the midst of a growth spurt will need fuel from food in order to keep developing.

As a rule of thumb, however, you can take it that, when your child's stomach is empty, it's about as big as their closed fist. You are now probably looking at your child's fist, thinking, 'That's tiny.' And you are right. It is a small space and it doesn't take much to fill it.

It's no wonder that we often misjudge the amount of food that our children are going to need to eat. The evidence of our miscalculation can be seen every day in the huge portions that we put out in front of children. Despite the fact that we have probably guessed wrong about how much space there is to be filled, it doesn't stop us from insisting that they eat it all.

Other factors, apart from the size of our stomachs, will also influence how much food we feel like eating at any one time. If, for example, you are feeling stressed and anxious, it's quite likely that you will 'lose your appetite'. That doesn't mean that you suddenly stopped needing to eat, it just means that for whatever reason your stomach gives your brain a message that it doesn't have the capacity to cope with a lot of food. Of course, in reality it's probably due to the fact that the adrenalin released with our anxiety shifts the flow of blood away from organs like your stomach and into major organs like your heart and lungs and your muscles. Digestion of food becomes a low priority, instinctively, if you are anticipating some threat or task that leaves you feeling anxious.

Equally, when you are very busy and task-focused doing something, it's easy not to notice any signals from your stomach that it is empty and needs to be refilled. So, while hunger messages are there, we don't necessarily respond to them. However, I would be fairly willing to bet that as soon as the project or task is finished, you will start to feel hungry and you will eat.

The exact same process is true for children. When they are nervous, anxious, busy or excited, food and hunger are often the last things on their mind. That doesn't mean that they need to be reminded and forced to eat; it just means that we need to be patient and trust that, when they do notice the hunger pangs. thev will come and eat.

When your child's stomach is empty, it's about as big as their closed fist

LITTLE AND OFTEN – THE KEY TO GOOD EATING HABITS

When it comes to food and eating little and often is probably the best policy. This includes at mealtimes. If you put out very small portions of food on your child's plate, it's much more likely that they will eat it all, and then they may even feel a sense of satisfaction at having cleared their plate. If you put a lot of food out on their plate and they only eat a small bit of it, they may feel guilty and under pressure because they know of your expectations that it all should be eaten. There is nothing wrong with a child having a very small first portion and then a very small second portion and then, if they still feel hungry, a third, fourth, fifth or sixth portion. It's much better that you eat, feel like you have finished and then judge whether you want more rather then eating, feeling full, but continuing to eat anyway just because the food is there in front of you. This is more likely to encourage over-eating than healthy eating.

If you regularly find that your child eats half of what you put out for them, then reduce their portion size by 50 per cent. Their behaviour in leaving half the food is trying to tell you about how much they instinctively feel they need. By cutting down the amount offered at the first sitting you are respectfully showing them that you heard. So when in doubt, watch your portion sizes.

WHERE THE TROUBLE BEGINS

As I mentioned earlier, the trouble with food begins because of our own misunderstandings and misperceptions about what is normal and regular for our children. If you remember, I talked about the fact that we need food in order to live, to grow and to move. We often assume, therefore, because our children are growing frantically, they must need huge amounts of food. Equally, because our children are so busy running hither and thither, they must also need huge amounts of food. The reality, of course, is that neither of these facts is as true as we believe. Yes, children are growing and certainly in the first year of life they grow at a very fast pace. But between the ages of one and six years they actually grow relatively slowly. Of course, between one and six years they become more active, but even their activity levels use up less energy than the equivalent activity of an adult. This is because their body size is so small, and it doesn't take as much energy to keep it moving. Despite this, we have a belief that a two-year-old should be eating more than a one-year-old, a four-year-old should be eating more that a two-year-old. In reality, a two-year-old probably eats proportionally less than a nine-month-old.

> If you put out very small portions of food on your child's plate, it's much more likely that they will eat it all, and then they may even feel a sense of satisfaction at having cleared their plate

Because of our belief that children need to eat in order to grow we sometimes start the process of weaning on to solids too soon. Six months of age is the earliest that you should begin to think about weaning your child from breast milk or formula on to solid food. Earlier than this, their stomachs aren't ready, and their digestive systems find it harder to cope with the solid food. This means that, when they eat solid food, they may well be getting a pain in their tummies. If that happens, then they could associate eating solid food with pain and so may become resistant or reluctant to eat. Also, babies will instinctively recognize that their mother's milk is higher in calories (and therefore will give them more energy for growth) than the equivalent volume of puréed vegetables.

Because, as I have mentioned earlier, their tummies are so small, they know that they need concentrated foods that are high in calories but low in volume. So, while a baby may be interested to try a few bites of vegetables that are rich in minerals and vitamins, they know that this is not a substitute for milk. Often, babies of this age might refuse to eat large portions of solid food simply because they know that they need more milk, which probably has three times the calorific value and therefore three times the energy that they need in order to keep growing. So the key to introducing solids is: don't start too early and don't be tempted to substitute solid food for breast

> In reality, a two-year-old probably eats proportionally less than a nine-month-old

milk or bottles too soon. If you do either of these things, your baby is likely to grumble, fuss and even refuse to eat. This, then, is just the start of the fighting, and so your child builds up a resistance to fruit, vegetables and other solid foods, not because they don't like them, but because they become associated with the fighting.

WHEN A CHILD'S GROWTH SLOWS DOWN, THEIR HUNGER GOES DOWN, TOO

Another key time at which problems emerge is about one year of age. Most children, somewhere between nine and eighteen months of age, will stop eating. They stop eating because they realize that their growth has slowed down so dramatically that they no longer need the same amount of food. In terms of what they need food for, it has reverted to just a small amount of growth, a small amount of activity and living. Most of us, however, are caught unawares by this. We don't expect a healthy one-year-old to suddenly stop eating and we can't understand why. This, then, may be the time when we begin to try all the tricks of the trade in order to cajole and persuade our child to eat more. This persuasion becomes the norm for our interaction with our child over food.

Interestingly, at around this time children also show an increased interest in feeding themselves. It's almost as if they know that they need to take responsibility now for what goes in or else they might end up being over-fed. Of course, when a one-year-old decides to feed himself, this is a slow and messy business and probably means that less food will go in. Some parents simply don't have the patience for this and so for either haste or ease they continue to feed (or over-feed) their child. If a child is continually fed by someone else they will lose interest in feeding themselves and – surprise, surprise – at age two or three they continue to show little interest in feeding themselves. This is frustrating for parents, who, again, often don't realize that they have set up this pattern of behaviour from their child. It is easy to see where conflict can begin once a parent gets frustrated with the fact that their child won't eat on their own. 'He won't eat unless I feed him' is a very common complaint. Of course, in most cases he won't eat because he has never had the opportunity to feed himself.

Babies who know what, how much and when they want to eat have only three things that they can do in order to prevent themselves from being over-fed. In the first instance they will close their mouth and turn their head to the side. This is a very clear communication from a child or baby that they don't want to eat. Unfortunately, due either to the parent's fear that the child won't eat or their mistaken assumption that the child needs to eat, they will force the issue. With a bit of persistence most mothers try to get past the initial blockage by distracting their child or in some other way tricking them to open their mouth.

When a one-year-old decides to feed himself, this is a slow and messy business

If a baby is really determined not to eat, however, they will then simply hold the food in their month and either spit it out or refuse to swallow. Usually, there is very little one can do to make a baby swallow food, and so the wait while your baby does not swallow becomes infuriating or distressing or both.

If a parent can somehow manage to get their child to swallow food that the child didn't want (and some parents can be very insistent), the last line of defence for a baby is to throw up. Unfortunately, most of the time, these cues that our children give off are misinterpreted simply as a bold refusal to eat. Often this is because we don't recognize that, for some of the reasons that I have outlined above, our babies don't have the need to eat.

MY FAVOURITE SOLUTION FOR CHILDREN WHO DON'T EAT

In my early days as a psychologist, before I realized the true dynamic that goes on between children and their parents over food, I would have supported parents in trying to force their child to eat. While I never advocated physical force-feeding, I certainly used to give advice about ways in which parents could cajole or deceive their child into eating food. I like to think that, because I am human, it's OK for me to have made this mistake. Now my advice to parents who are fighting with their children over food is to simply stop their fighting.

When I suggest the method to parents, it sounds easy in theory, but actually the practice of it is very hard. By the time most parents come looking for help about their child's 'problem eating', the patterns of conflict are well established and parents' stress levels about food have usually gone through the roof. If eating or not eating food has become a battle of wills between you and your child, then you are probably finding that it's one of the few areas where your child's will is prevailing. This is because most children know that there are a few things in this world that they do have full control over; one of those things is what goes into their bodies and another is what comes out.

A new approach is needed. That new approach needs to be based on the

My advice to parents who are fighting with their children over food is to simply stop their fighting

understanding that children, if left alone, will regulate their own food intake to ensure that they are not left hungry and that they will get enough energy to live, grow and move. Unfortunately, for most of us adults, it's quite a leap of faith to actually believe this. We find it almost impossible to accept that a child will regulate their own food intake. We struggle to believe that they will eat a large enough quantity and variety of food. But you can take it from me that they will. I don't promise that if you start giving your children freedom about what, when and how much they eat that they will suddenly start eating more. I do promise that they won't dramatically lose weight and become unwell. In practice, most children left to their own devices will continue to eat the same amount, and possibly the same variety, of food. They just eat them without stress.

To support your child in this it's really important for you to have a range and a variety of foods available for your child. All of the foods must be healthy, and you are probably going to have to ban sweets, chocolate and crisps, as these are not the snacks for your child to graze on if they feel peckish.

As long as you never refuse to give your child food when they look for it, they will not lose weight

So, depending on the age of your child, you might want to sit them down and explain to them that things are going to be different from now on. You can explain that you are no longer going to try to feed them, you are no longer going to try to verbally encourage them and you are no longer going to plead with them to eat. Rather, you will be offering them small amounts of food at mealtimes, and they can choose to eat or not eat as they see fit.

It's really important that you do make food available to your child at other times even if they are not eating at mealtimes. This strategy is not 'they can only eat at mealtimes or otherwise they will starve'. It's possible that, if children were offered no other food at any time of the day other than mealtimes, they would choose to eat at mealtimes. However, I don't think it's right or moral to intentionally deprive children of food.

The strategy of giving your child a truly free choice about food does work. As I said, it doesn't encourage your child to eat more and it doesn't lead to them suddenly wanting to sit down and have a full meal with the family at dinnertime. What it does lead to is no conflict, no stress and healthier attitudes to food in children. A child who is no longer being forced to eat will come to enjoy the food that they are eating rather than feel stressed by it. Finally they are being given the chance to eat food because they want it and not because they must have it.

WHEN YOU GIVE YOUR CHILD THE RIGHT TO CHOOSE WHEN AND WHAT TO EAT, RESIST THE URGE TO INTERFERE

Of course, in order to sustain a strategy like this, parents need to be willing to commit to it 100 per cent and not deviate from it. This will mean biting your tongue on many an occasion when you would be otherwise ready to encourage, cajole, plead or threaten your child to eat the food. It's actually stopping these kinds of behaviours that parents find most difficult. Usually, because they have done it for years, they find it very hard to stop forcing their child. In the chapter on feelings I go into quite a lot of detail about stress management

> A child who is no longer being forced to eat will come to enjoy the food that they are eating rather than feel stressed by it

and about staying in charge of your own feelings. This would be good information for you to read again before you start a programme of not forcing your child to eat.

When you give your child the freedom to eat or not to eat, you can be pretty sure that in the early stages they will choose not to eat. Don't be disheartened. Continue to offer small amounts of food at every mealtime and then be warm-hearted in offering other foods later if your child requests it. This isn't the time to start bending over backwards and cooking an alternative meal for your child. If they are hungry later you can offer then whatever was offered earlier (if that's what they want) or something else that doesn't involve any preparation or cooking. This might be a piece of fruit, a yogurt, a cracker, some bread, some nuts, some dried fruit or any other healthy snack that you can think of or that you have to hand when they ask.

Remember, if, when you put out a portion of food on your child's plate, you notice that they consistently only eat half of it, then in future put out only that half amount. That way you won't waste food by putting it on your child's plate knowing that they are not going to eat it. Do keep remembering that children's tummies are small and their appetites may not be big.

You may become concerned that your child will lose weight if you stop forcing them to eat. Based on your experience you may believe that, if you don't get the food into them, it won't go in at all. I am confident, however, that, as long as you never refuse to give your child food when they look for it, they will not lose weight. If you follow the programme that I am suggesting, where you offer your child small amounts of food without any pressure to eat it, then you will probably find that they will actually put on weight as well as becoming more relaxed, more adventurous and happier about what they are eating.

Remember, if, when you put out a portion of food on your child's plate, you notice that they consistently only eat half of it, then in future put out only that half amount

MEALTIMES

For parents who have issues with their children's eating, mealtimes are often the battle ground where bitter and distressing conflicts are played out for the whole family to endure. In our culture mealtimes have become quite ritualized. They tend to happen at the same time every day. Most families with busy schedules will have times for breakfast, lunch, dinner and supper. This doesn't give much scope for flexibility when it comes to deciding when to eat. Usually the decision is made for children.

Contrary to what you might be expecting, I actually think it is a good thing, however, that there are set mealtimes. For all of their inflexibility, I think mealtimes are an important social gathering, and if we didn't gather for mealtimes it's possible

Mealtimes are an important social gathering

that many families might not stop and be together as a group at any stage. What I'd like you to consider now is that you make your mealtimes about having a good social and emotional connection with your child and not about what and how much they are eating.

This could be a big shift for many parents to make. If you are stuck in a downward-turning spiral of fights, refusals, pleadings, ignorings and stress at mealtimes, it can take a mammoth reversal of attitude to create a light, good-humoured and easy-going meal experience. You have to move from trying to emotionally or physically force your child to eat to believing that, left to their own devices, they will eat enough. You need to see your role as being to make food and eating a pleasant experience rather than being to ensure that a certain minimum number of calories gets ingested. One opportunity to make food a pleasant experience is at mealtimes.

Preparing and serving food can be a communal and very fun affair, although your patience in coping with the helping hands from small children will often determine how much you are able to tolerate 'communality' in getting a meal ready. It's good to involve children from a young age in the preparation of a meal. You'd be surprised at how accomplished they can get at spooning, pouring, measuring and even cutting. If you find that you can't tolerate their assistance with cooking, then you can make sure that they can be involved in the setting of the table, whether that is laying out mats for under the plates or setting out cutlery or crockery. When children are a part of the preparation, they are more likely to feel part of the meal too.

A TIME TO TALK

Increasing the social aspect of meals involves trying to include everybody at the table. This means pulling babies in high chairs close so they are part of the group as opposed to sitting outside the group. It might also mean having a plan in your own head of topics to talk about. This can include reminiscing about the activities of the day; making plans for later in the day or the next day; discussing what happened at playtimes; talking about school, friends, teachers, uncles, aunts; remembering things from your own childhood; telling stories about when your children were younger ... the list is endless.

This is a great opportunity to use all of the skills I discussed in the chapter on communication, especially the skills of active listening, to encourage your children to talk back. In fact, I would urge you to talk about anything except the food on the table. If you have been struggling with fussy eating, then the chances are that you are over-vigilant about and over-involved in the food that your child has in front of them.

> In fact, I would urge you to talk about anything except the food on the table

Once you start eating, you may find that there are more habits that you need to change. For example, with small children it's not worth getting hung up on whether cutlery is used to eat their meal. Yes, it's a bonus if your two-year-old uses a spoon and a fork, but is it really a bad thing if they choose to eat with their fingers? If you want to promote a relaxed attitude to food, for example, then maybe having a fight over whether their cutlery is used or not is not worth it.

I recognize that, if you are giving your child the real freedom to choose to eat or not eat, then it is quite likely that they will choose not to eat. It's very disheartening sometimes when food that you have taken the time and the trouble to prepare is refused by your child. We can take their choice not to eat 'our food' very personally. Often because we have invested so much time and energy in ensuring that they get enough food and enough nutrition to keep them healthy we take it as a personal insult when they claim not to like it. It is as if they are giving us an underlying message that they don't love us because they won't eat our food. Of course, we can only believe that they don't love us by not eating because we have imbued the food with that meaning. It's really hard, but really important, not to get angry if food is refused.

Irrespective of how much or how little has been eaten you decide on a reasonable time frame for your meal, maybe ten to twenty minutes, and then after that time anybody who has had enough to eat can be excused from the table. Before that, it's worth encouraging children to stay at the table even if they are not hungry, simply so that they can be involved in the social dimension of the meal. You can explain that even if they don't want to eat, it's good for them to hang out with their family to chat and to share stories of the day.

A WORD ABOUT SNACKING

One of the difficulties that lots of parents find themselves in is that they invest a lot in mealtimes and then don't really pay attention to what their children eat at other times of the day. At the moment, I think there is a huge problem with the amount of sugary, processed and unhealthy treats and snacks that children have the opportunity to eat. Most children, if given a choice, will choose foods that are higher in sugar or salt content rather than foods that are lower. Offer most children the choice between an apple and a bar of chocolate, and they will first choose the bar of chocolate. They are not making their choice on the basis of health, nutrition or dietary requirements, they are making it because they prefer the taste of chocolate.

I am all for children snacking and grazing during the day. I would much prefer children to eat what they want when they want rather than only being allowed to eat at mealtimes, but if they are going to graze and snack, then I do think it's crucial that the snacks available to them are healthy. I spoke to a mum once who complained to me that her son 'eats nothing'. When I started talking to her about the issue, I discovered that her son eats almost nothing at mealtimes but was quite happy to take a packet of crisps and a bar of chocolate or a packet of sweets from their 'goodies' press at all times of the day. This was not a child eating nothing. This was simply a child eating too much of the wrong thing and not feeling hungry for foods that were better and more healthy for him.

The obvious solution for that particular family was to clear out their 'goodies' press so that there were no more sweet treats available in the house. Her son never really ate much more, and continued to eat very little at mealtimes, but his mum was able to change her attitude so that she saw that, as long as he was eating snacks such as cheese, crackers, fruit and cereals at other times of the day, she could rest assured that he was getting a healthy and balanced enough diet and wouldn't fade away and die.

KEY POINTS TO REMEMBER

- Normal eating habits vary widely; indeed, it can seem as if there is no such thing as a normal eating habit.

- Babies and small children will experience a biological imperative to eat, as they instinctively know that they must eat to live, grow and move.

- Equally, however, children will also know when they don't want or need to eat.

- Expect children to stop, or dramatically reduce, their food intake at about one year of age.

- The problems between parents and children about food often begin because we misunderstand or misinterpret children's reasons for not eating.

- We believe them to be bold, resistant, oppositional, fussy or picky, even though they are trying to tell us that they have had enough or don't need the food we are offering.

- Babies turning their heads away, holding food in their mouths, spitting it out or throwing up are all sure signs that they don't need the food you are offering when you are offering it.

- Children will regulate their own food intake if they are given the opportunity to do so.

- If you fight with your child about food, then consider stopping the fighting.

- Give your child a free choice about eating or not as they choose.

- Continue to offer them small amounts of food at regular intervals but don't force them to eat if they don't want to.

- Forcing children to eat includes pleading, cajoling, tricking, demanding, bribing and physically forcing them.

- If they are choosing not to eat at mealtimes, for example, then make sure there are other healthy snacks available to them at other times of the day.

- You don't need to turn your house into a 'cook-on-demand' restaurant, but avoid restricting food just because a dinner wasn't eaten.

- Make mealtimes into a social occasion more than a food-cramming occasion.

- Encourage everyone to sit together; just don't expect everyone to eat.

- Involve children in the preparation of food so that they can develop positive attitudes to the food, even if they don't want to eat it.

- If you are going to encourage snacking, then make sure it is healthy foods – if in doubt empty your 'treats' press and get rid of crisps, sweets and sugary drinks so that nobody can be tempted.

- Having a child who eats a small amount and variety of foods happily is a better outcome than having a child who eats more food under great stress.

9

NEGOTIATING CHILDCARE, PRE-SCHOOL AND SCHOOL

SUPPORTING YOUR CHILD'S CONNECTIONS TO THE OUTSIDE WORLD

We often forget that other people look after our children because we are so absorbed in looking after them ourselves and also in keeping our families running. Sometimes we hand our children over into someone else's care with a painful wrench and sometimes with a grateful sigh. We trust others to mind, stimulate, engage, support, encourage, develop and educate them on our behalf. Giving over the care of your child to someone else is a major step. For some of us it happens when they are just a few months old, and we have to return to work. For others it will be when they are going to pre-school or school, sometime between the ages of three and five years. No matter when it happens, it is still a big deal.

Both necessity and personal choice drive the decisions to place our children in childcare, pre-schools and schools. If you must work, for example, then you have no choice about using childcare. Some people don't have to work and so they get to choose between staying at home with their own children and going out to work. With the financial pressures on many families now this choice can seem like a luxury.

Sometimes, we have a choice about where they go; other times, there is just one option. We still have to negotiate and reach common understanding with whomever it is that has charge of our child, no matter how, and where, they end up. At times this can be straightforward and easy and at times it can be fraught with difficulty and stress for you or your child.

THIS CHAPTER LOOKS AT ...

⇢ **Choosing your childcare if you have a choice**

⇢ **Negotiating with teachers and childcare providers**

⇢ **Separation anxiety at the start of pre-school or school**

⇢ **Reinforcing learning and developing good homework habits**

CHOOSING CHILDCARE

Having a choice about childcare is a luxury. When that choice includes having one or other parent stay at home with your own children, it is especially luxurious. Even if one parent can't stay with their child, it is nice, too, to have a choice about which of several alternative options you will opt for. For example, you may have a choice about which crèche to go for, or whether to have a crèche or a relative to mind your child.

I lay my cards on the table early: I believe it's best for children to have one of their own parents mind them rather than anybody else. It's almost impossible to expect any other person to care as much or to go as far in the care of your child as you would yourself. Even though other people can certainly care very deeply about and love your child, and can want to do the very best for them, it is very rare that it would be as much as you would do yourself. As a general rule, parents would be more patient, more tolerant and more understanding of their own child than another carer would be.

> I believe it's best for children to have one of their own parents mind them rather than anybody else

Lots of families have their children cared for by other people out of necessity and also out of personal choice. The most common options for alternative childcare are to have your child minded by his or her grandparents; by a childminder in your own home; by a childminder in their home; in a crèche; or by an au-pair. All of these options have advantages and disadvantages.

GRANDPARENTS

If you are lucky enough to have your parents or your partner's parents living locally, then having them mind your child can be a good option. In the first instance, your child will know their grandparents, and so it will be an easy transition for them to be minded by them. If it's your own parents, then you will know clearly what kind of care your child will receive. Assuming that you are happy enough with your own upbringing, then you can be reassured to know that your child will be happy and well cared for.

Grandparents also tend to be more sensitive to your wishes about how children should be reared. So, for example, if you have a particular way of doing things, then your parents are more likely to implement that in your absence than might be possible in somewhere like a crèche. Another benefit of having grandparents minding your child is that, if your child gets sick, they are probably more likely to cope with that and not have to call you out of work to come and take your son.

On the flip side, if your son is a very busy toddler and your parents are older, then you may find that they don't have quite the same energy to keep up with him as you might have. The other real difficulty is that most grandparents fall into the role of being a grandparent with delight. They like the fact that they don't normally have to mind their grandchildren but instead they can treat them and spoil them a little bit. This could prove a bit of a problem, however, if they become a main carer for your son. In that instance they have to revert into a parent role, setting and enforcing rules and limits, when they might prefer not to have to do that.

CHILDMINDER IN THEIR OWN HOME

Another option is to have your child minded by a childminder in their home. The advantages to this are that your child would be in family surroundings and would probably have a very sociable environment, particularly if the childminder has their own children.

When your child is a baby, then having them minded by a minder can also be really helpful because they will probably get one-to-one attention that they may not get in somewhere like a crèche. Also, because your child is with a minder in their home, and if you get on well with them, the arrangement can often be quite flexible, so that, if you run late, it's not a huge imposition for your child to stay on that bit longer. Similarly, just as with grandparents, providing that your relationship with the minder is good, it's quite likely that they will be able to care for your child even if your child gets sick.

Assuming that you are happy enough with your own upbringing, then you can be reassured to know that your child will be happy and well cared for

Some of the disadvantages to having your child minded in a minder's home are that, when you come to do the pick-up, it can be very disruptive for your child. If they have been in a warm, cosy family environment for the day, and you come to pick them up in the cold dark of a winter's evening, they can be very reluctant to leave. So, rather than being met with open arms, you end up being faced with a minor tantrum. Also, your child is quite likely to be engrossed in some activity and not want to be parted from it.

CHILDMINDER IN YOUR HOME

Having a childminder come to your home to look after your little baby is another good option. Your child then has the familiarity of their home environment and they don't ever have to get used to or adjust to new surroundings. Also, in the morning, if your start is early, then they don't even have to be disrupted and woken up to be brought out to wherever they are going to be minded. Logistically, for you, this makes it all much simpler. Even when you come home, that transition will be easier because you are not going to be disrupting your child to the same extent.

One of the difficulties that may arise, however, is that if the childminder has different rules to you then this might cause conflict and confusion for your child. Children can be very adaptable and can understand that there is one set of rules in one place and another set of rules in another place. However, when there are two sets of rules that are used in the one place, it can be a bit more confusing. Also, depending on the childminder, it's possible that your child won't get exposed to as many different social situations as they might if they are going out to somebody else's home or to a crèche.

CRÈCHE

Having your child minded in a crèche means that you have the comfort of a well-regulated sector of childcare. The carers working in that environment will have a professional knowledge of children and their development, and good crèches will conform to the strict guidelines that are there for the care of children. That means that good standards of care must be maintained. Most crèches are also very well stocked with age-appropriate activities and play materials. It's quite likely that a crèche will have a very routined day for your child which is also comforting and will allow them to become confident and settled.

Crèches, by their nature, care for a large number of children. As a result, it's possible that your child won't get the same level of one-to-one attention that they might get in other childcare arrangements. Some children may find that the highly social environment of a crèche, where there are lots of other children around, competing for attention, space and materials, is a little too challenging. Also, because a crèche has to cater for a range of children with a range of needs, they may not be able to employ the same kinds of management techniques that you use at home.

AU-PAIR

Finally, having an au-pair mind your child could be an option. The benefit of having an au-pair minding your child is that they are going to bring a fresh and new culture to your family. However, beyond that there are not many other advantages. When you seek an au-pair, it's very difficult to be able to have a sense of who they are and what kind of childcare experience they are bringing. You have no way of telling what their priority is going to be when they arrive. For them, the experience may be about the opportunity to learn English and to hang out in a new country, where minding children is a secondary and tiresome chore. Also, au-pairs tend to come and go quite quickly. So even if an au-pair is very good, it's likely that, after a few months, they are going to be moving on, and then your child is left trying to readjust and attach to a new carer. Really, au-pairing is best seen as having an extra pair of hands to assist you at home. It's not a good idea to rely on au-pairs as your main form of childcare. It's a bit too much of a gamble.

Whatever kind of childcare you decide is the best (or only) option for your child then it's really important to continue to monitor how that seems to be going for them. You need to stay attuned to their moods and to their behaviour as an indicator of their happiness or dissatisfaction with the particular care they are getting. If your child is continually fractious and resists going to childcare, it is possible that they are struggling with some aspect of the care that they are getting. Without the language to explain it to you they would probably be relying on you noticing how unhappy they are in order to make a change. At that point, if you are concerned about some aspect of the care that your child is receiving, then you need to be able to talk about it with the minder. So let's look at how best to communicate with the person who is caring for your child.

NEGOTIATING WITH TEACHERS AND CHILDCARE PROVIDERS

Giving your child over to someone else to be minded and cared for is a big deal. If it's the case that you have to work, then daily childminding for your baby or toddler is a necessity, and you are going to have to deal regularly with whomever it is that is minding them. It is great if it is a family member or a friend whom you already trust. The chances are that in those situations you are going to find it easy to talk about your baby and to explain how you want her to be cared for. However, sometimes when the minder already has lots of childrearing experience it can be tricky negotiating how you want your baby minded. If your baby's granny, for example, already has strong and fixed ideas about childrearing, then your opinion, especially as a first-time parent, may not be listened to. You may have to work hard to be heard.

If it's the case that your child has joined a large and busy crèche, you may find it difficult in the early days to get a clear sense of who is actually minding your child. Make it your business, however, to find out who is actually responsible for your child. Even if you never have a problem or issue to discuss, you will still want to know who will be in the best position to give you a report at the end of each day about how your child has got on. Certainly, in most crèches, they will be keeping a written record of the different activities and events of the child's day.

Whatever kind of childcare you decide is the best (or only) option for your child then it's really important to continue to monitor how that seems to be going for them

For babies, for example, they will probably have a record of how many feeds your baby had and how many wet or dirty nappies your baby produced. They will also have recorded how much sleep your baby has had over the course of the day. This basic information is vital for you to know in planning your evening so that, if your baby is crying, you can know what is likely to be the reason. If they fed her just before you picked her up, for example, then hunger is less likely than wind to be the cause of her distress.

However, sometimes when the minder already has lots of childrearing experience it can be tricky negotiating how you want your baby minded

What can really add to the report of the day is some sense of how your baby got on with the people minding them. For example, were they fretful and fractious or calm and settled? Did they cry a lot or a little during the day? When they cried was someone able to go to them? Did they settle quickly when they were comforted by someone? Did they enjoy being cuddled more than being put down on their own?

The same questions are also relevant for older children. How did they get on in the group that they were in? Did they play alone or with another child or children? How did they negotiate the use of toys? Did they have a nap during the day? How was their appetite when it came to food? Were they complaining of any aches or pains?

GETTING THE TIMING RIGHT

Of course, answering all these questions takes time. You need to check the system in your child's crèche for the best time to have this kind of a chat. Almost everybody who minds children is only too delighted to talk with parents about the children in their care. The only thing you need to bear in mind as parents is that your timing needs to be good. For example, if there is an issue or problem that you would like to bring up, then don't expect to be able to just raise it at the end of a long day; rather you may be better making an appointment to meet separately with the minder at some other more suitable time. You need to remember, for example, that, if a crèche is very busy with lots of other children still there when you're coming to pick up your child, nobody may be free to talk at length to you about how your child got on. Sometimes, this is another benefit of your child being minded by a childminder or a relative. A 'home' minder will often have more time to spend with you talking about how your child got on during the day.

The same is true if your child is in pre-school or school. Most teachers, while they may be happy to chat quickly about a child, often will not have the time to talk at length at the end of the school day; they may have their own children who are waiting to be picked up somewhere else.

The other big difficulty that occurs when parents go to talk to minders or teachers is that they forget that the minder or teacher has more than simply their child to care for. So, while your little darling is top of your own priority list, he or she may not be top of the priority list for the teacher. This is another good reason to give a teacher some advance notice of the fact that you would like to talk to them about your child.

It you have a complaint about some aspect of the care that your child is receiving, then it can be very stressful for you and for the minder/teacher when that needs to be addressed. As a parent, you need to be ready for the fact that the minder or teacher

If you have a criticism of an aspect of your child's care, you need to be careful not to sound blaming or accusatory

may, initially, be quite defensive if they perceive that you are in some way criticizing their role with your child. Sometimes it can be really helpful to say at the start if your issue doesn't involve the teacher directly. The teacher is more likely to be at their ease if they feel that they are not going to be personally attacked. You also need to be careful, if you do have criticism of some aspect of the care being offered, that you don't sound blaming or accusatory. However you have managed to hear about the problem, you need to remember that it's only one side of the story. The teacher or minder will have their side of the story, and you need to be ready to listen to that. If you go in all guns blazing you may just alienate the teacher or minder, they will go on the defensive, and any hope of having an open discussion and reaching a resolution may be lost.

WHEN YOUR CHILD IS CAUSING DIFFICULTIES

Often, the shoe is on the other foot, too. We may get asked to meet with the teacher or minder because our child is the one who is causing some difficulty. The most common problem in schools, pre-schools and crèches is when a child's behaviour becomes difficult or oppositional. This can be a very hard thing to hear from somebody else. You may not have had any difficulties at home, and so it can come as a bit of a shock to the system to find out that somebody else who is minding them is struggling to cope with some aspect of their behaviour.

One reason for this mismatch is often that your child, who copes very well in the one-to-one environment of your home, struggles when that attention is divided amongst many. It's quite possible in this situation that your child will then begin to act out their frustration at not getting enough attention, and this could lead them into conflict with their minder or teacher. Much as teachers and minders like to be able to give your child 100 per cent of their attention, you need to remember that it's just not possible.

If you go in all guns blazing you may just alienate the teacher or minder and they will go on the defensive

Another possible reason is that your child might be trying to come to terms with a new management system, and their behaviour is just an expression of the confusion or anxiety about that difference.

Of course, even when you and the teacher or minder have a very good working relationship, you can come into conflict over the suggested way of dealing with whatever is the issue. Again, certain kinds of behaviour-management strategies may be very effective at home but just are not applicable in a large group setting. Also, certain rules might need to be adhered to in a school or pre-school that you wouldn't choose to have in your home. Often, if you can manage to have an open and frank discussion about your parenting style and the management style of the school or crèche, you will find that there is a lot of common ground, and you can reach some agreement that might provide a little bit of consistency between home and the crèche, pre-school or school.

If you need to have a proper discussion or meeting with your child's teacher or minder, then reread the chapter on communication. Remember all your listening skills. Remember to try and empathize with the position of the teacher and not just the position of your child. Remember that it's possible to acknowledge somebody else's point of view even if you don't agree with it. For example, if somebody feels you have understood them, then they will cope better even if you don't agree with them. Just as when dealing with your own child, you need to stay in charge of your feelings when you are talking to your child's minder. If you lose your cool, then chances are you will end up saying things that will make the relationship worse between you. You being in conflict with their teacher or minder won't make the situation any better for your child.

Often if you can manage to have an open and frank discussion about your parenting style and the management style of the school or crèche, you will find that there is a lot of common ground

SEPARATION ANXIETY

Whether it is at the start of school or pre-school, those first days of leaving a parent at the gate or the door can be frightening times for a small child. The extent to which a child will experience separation anxiety is often determined by their temperament and personality and by yours. Some children are naturally robust, outgoing and gregarious. They love the excitement of meeting new people and engaging in new things. New environments such as schools or pre-schools are a challenge to be met and explored. They are adaptable and can cope easily with a new routine, new faces and new expectations of them.

Having a child who gets worried, stressed, upset and anxious at the thought or reality of leaving you is not a sign of failure

But if your child isn't like this, then they may actually find the newness and uncertainty of school to be overwhelming. It is natural that, at times of stress like this, a child would want to cling to what is secure and known. That point of security is you. Having a child who gets worried, stressed, upset and anxious at the thought or reality of leaving you is not a sign of failure. It is simply a sign that your child knows where to turn for comfort.

However, I would challenge you to think about yourself in the midst of the separation too. I would be willing to lay a bet that, if your child is anxious about a separation, you are too. Somewhere, either in your conscious or unconscious, you have fears and worries about your child doing OK and being OK in the new place. It can be hard to admit to it, especially when you are trying to put on a brave face for your child. It is natural for us too, though, to be worried about the ability of our children to cope with all of the pressures and newness of the situation. We know our children. We know how easy they find it to make friends, to participate in groups, to stick to rules and adapt to new routines. If our knowledge points to the fact that, actually, any or all of these things will be difficult for our child, then it makes sense to be a little worried.

The trouble is, however, that our children are very attuned to us too. They usually know how we feel and may indeed be better at intuitively picking up on our feelings than we are ourselves. As a result, if they pick up on our worry and anxiety, then they take it on for themselves. So, if your child sees you being worried, then they will wonder what it is about the new thing (school) that is worrying. Without a clear idea of what they face they will then build up an anxiety about the unknown. This anxiety may be entirely projected from you or it may be in tandem with their own natural anxiety as we discussed above.

This, then, presents a challenge to you, the parent, to be really in charge of your feelings. It is difficult enough for a child to be worrying on their own behalf; you certainly don't want them worrying on your behalf, too!

Let's look at a typical example of a child on the first day of school. We'll assume that separation anxiety is an issue. We are also going to assume that this is a parent who has prepared in order to try to minimize the impact of the anxiety.

Right from waking there is a hint of tension, maybe excitement, in the air. Over breakfast your five-year-old daughter is a little fractious and seems to be a bit narky with everyone. She refuses to put on her new uniform, claiming to hate the colour of her tracksuit (even though it was 'gorgeous' when it was being bought). In fairness to you, though, you are keeping your cool, because you recognize that she is possibly a bit worried about school starting and you remember that, when a child gets worried, they often act it out in difficult or bold behaviour.

> **It is difficult for a child to be worrying on their own behalf; you don't want them worrying about you too!**

You get straight in with a few empathy statements. 'You don't really seem to want to put on your uniform. I'm guessing you are probably feeling a bit excited and a bit worried about going to school today.' Or 'Once you put on your uniform, you will be almost ready for school, but I wonder if it doesn't feel like you are ready inside; I wonder if it actually feels a bit scary going to school.'

Amy, your daughter, responds with a shrug and turns her head away. You then say,

'I think going to school for the first time can be scary but I also know that it can be fun. I wonder what games your teacher will play with you today. I forget – what is your teacher called? I remember playing chasing in the yard on my first day at school. My teacher was a tall woman, just like yours. I felt a bit nervous until I met her in the class but then I felt OK. Are there more boys or girls in your class, I wonder? I'll bet they are all wondering what today will be like as well. Do you remember when you get your first break-time? Oh, it'll probably seem like a very fast day in school ...'

Basically, you keep up the patter, distracting your daughter so that she doesn't have time to actually think about the worry. I'd be amazed if you haven't helped her into her clothes and got her hair and teeth brushed while keeping you both diverted in this way. If the distracting patter is helping, then distract her all the way on the journey.

The only thing to remember, while chatting on, is to keep putting a positive spin on any school-based comments and to remain matter-of-fact and truthful about any school routines or rules. There is no point in lying to your child, because it will only add to their anxiety on subsequent days. If, for example, you tell them that they will only be in school a tiny, little time on the first day, they may get distressed or disappointed when they are there for an hour or however long it proves to be. That distress and disappointment will be as much with you for lying to them as with the reality of the school day. Equally, you can't tell them they will be sitting beside someone nice because you don't know if they

Keep putting a positive spin on any school-based comments and remain matter-of-fact and truthful about any school routines or rules

will or not. Don't make promises you can't keep either, like promising to wait outside until they are done! Amy needs to be able to trust you and she can't do that if you are not truthful with her, even if your lies are white ones designed to reassure her.

If you find that your chat isn't enough of a distraction, then do use other things to distract her as you get her ready. If distraction doesn't work at all, then you may have to be determined and just get her dressed and ready despite her protestations. You need to remember that it is probably worry and anxiety that are driving her upset and her tantrum. So keep empathizing with her about how hard it can be to go to school and how anxiety-provoking it can be. Let her know that you have confidence in her and the place she is going, and that no matter how upset she is she will be going anyway. This is not a time to wimp out and cave in to her emotional blackmail. Even if it is distressing, you have to keep going. Her anxiety is a temporary and natural thing, and she will be able to be OK once she gets used to the school.

This is not a time to wimp out and cave in to her emotional blackmail

THE BIG MOMENT ARRIVES

So you get to the school. Either you and Amy are calm enough because you have successfully distracted her, or she is very distressed, and you are not far behind. Hopefully, both you and Amy have been there before and have met the teacher in advance. That would be an ideal situation. In lots of cases, while you may have seen the school, you may not have had a chance to visit and meet anyone. I would encourage you to stay focused from the moment you arrive to the moment you go. Your focus should be on getting Amy to the classroom or the assigned meeting point for the class, handing her over to the teacher and then leaving. You need to keep this process moving all the time. The longer you delay or dawdle, the greater the opportunity for anxiety to rise.

When you get to the teacher and the introductions are made, then you turn to Amy and say, 'I love you, Amy, I'm so pleased you are taking this big step of going off to school. I know you will cope really well and I can't wait to hear all about it when I meet you at the gate at 11.30 (or whenever the end time of the first day is). Bye, bye, darling.' With a bit of luck Amy will say, 'Bye, bye,' out of habit, and then you need to go. If Amy doesn't immediately respond with a goodbye, then don't wait, turn on your heel and leave without looking back. If she is not saying goodbye, then she is probably winding up to say, 'Don't go, don't leave me,' with the associated tears. If you hang around and seem to be a bit undecided or uncertain about going, you can be sure that Amy will take the opportunity to start crying, or wailing, for you to stay and not leave her.

If Amy is upset, you need to have confidence that her teacher is able to cope with it. Teachers in pre-schools and in the reception classes of national schools are well practised and experienced in the art of comforting and distracting those children who do get upset. Invariably, the upset will last for just a couple of minutes at most, and then your child will get on with the task of adapting. If you hang around, trying to comfort your own child, it will only add to the upset and prevent the teacher from doing her job and sorting out your child's difficulty. Even if your daughter sounds distraught, you need to harden your heart a little and keep going out the door. This is definitely a time when your best intentions will inflame a situation rather than calm it. Liaising later with Amy's teacher and talking to friends who have experienced the same thing can give you the strength to keep going with confidence that you are doing the right thing.

With separation anxiety, it is important for your child to actually experience the separation and then to experience the comforting and realize that they are doing OK, even though they are apart from you. If you don't separate, then they can't move on. Listening outside the door or waiting at the school gate count as not separating! Give your child a chance and leave completely.

When you do come back for the pick-up, check with the teacher, out of earshot of your child, about how she got on. With Amy, later, review the morning and focus on the positives only. Acknowledge it if she says she was upset but don't dwell on it. By all means understand with her that it probably seemed scary at first, but then she did so many fun things.

Don't be disheartened, either, if you find that the seemingly traumatic moments of bereft crying are repeated for a few days or even a week or more. Even for the most well-adjusted children it takes time to get used to a new environment. We need to stay steadfast and relaxed about both the reality of having to go and the awareness that this, too, will pass. And it does pass, I promise, as long as you stay calm, determined and understanding with your child.

Even for the most well-adjusted children it takes time to get used to a new environment

Some parents find that their child will go happily on the first day, oblivious to the reality of school, and then the resistance to going comes on the next and subsequent days.

The only way to deal with school resistance is to stay firm and determined that your child will go to school. Be aware and empathize with their feelings, for sure, but don't let their anxieties persuade you to keep them home. Your confidence with their teacher and their school will be enormously supportive to them in making the transition to school.

DEVELOPING GOOD HOMEWORK HABITS AND ENCOURAGING LEARNING

I and my family have chosen to follow a completely different educational system to the mainstream primary education. Not that this was always the case. My eldest child spent two years in national school. He really enjoyed his time there, but we made a decision to offer him a different educational experience. So for his first two years at school we did the homework thing with him.

My children now attend a Steiner-Waldorf school, Raheen Wood School, in East Clare. In that system, formal education as you know it in primary school doesn't start until a child is about seven years of age. Prior to that, children attend Kindergarten, and the focus is on rhythm and flow to the day and the week, connections to nature and other people and play – unstructured, imaginative and exploratory play. Even in the older classes, while the children do 'academic' work and learn reading, writing and arithmetic, they do so

Homework needs to be a habit for a child in order for it to be easy

through a very different curriculum that focuses on the holistic development of children. My children love it and not least because there is no homework for the younger classes.

However, I realize that I and my family are in a minority. Almost all children are in mainstream school, and that means that they are all getting homework. Homework can be a real challenge for children and parents alike.

Homework needs to be a habit for a child in order for it to be easy. Habits are born out of routine, and so I would encourage you to start early to develop a routine for your child when they begin school. Essentially, what you are doing is organizing their afternoon or early evening to ensure that there is a consistent time, place and method for approaching homework.

The kind of routine I would suggest involves coming in from school and having a snack and a chat about the day. Straight afterwards your child should be getting their bag, emptying out their lunch things and getting their books out on to the table.

I think with small children it works best to have them at the kitchen table, where you can keep an eye on them and keep them focused more easily. Always start homework with a check of the tasks to do. Generally there will be a small bit of reading or letter recognition, some counting or number recognition and a small bit of colouring or writing. It is useful to always tackle the tasks in the same order as this will bring habit and familiarity to the homework process.

It is great if your child has a natural interest in things academic and if they enjoy homework tasks. If not, then you will probably find that you have to work hard to help maintain your child's enthusiasm and attention on the tasks at hand. Try to avoid being punitive when it comes to homework. If you find that you are having to use threats of consequences to get your child to focus and stay with their homework, then you are on a slippery slope to creating a very negative attitude in your child's mind about homework and maybe even academic work in general.

It is best to use verbal encouragement and praise as the motivators to keep your child going. You may find that your child has no difficulty achieving the tasks but just doesn't have the concentration span required to stick at it. Whenever you turn your back they drift off into a dream world, and the pen and paper sit there untouched. This is really common for five- and six-year-olds. If this is so, you might like to try timing the tasks as a motivation. Making the tasks a race against the clock can add enough spice to make them interesting, and it may appeal to the competitive nature of some children. If you put a challenge to your child to complete the task by the time you have counted to ten, you may find that they rise to it admirably.

LIKE EVERYTHING, THE KEY TO GETTING USED TO HOMEWORK IS ROUTINE

It is your responsibility to ensure that conflict about homework is kept to a bare minimum. For a five- or six-year-old the imposition of homework can be just as frustrating as any of their daily tasks. You need to remember this and be prepared to empathize while still ensuring that they stay in the routine and get into the habit of sitting down regularly. Same place, same time and same procedure will encourage this, but often it is your enthusiasm for the benefits of homework that will carry your child through the tasks.

Your enthusiasm can also be used to role-model both effective homework routines and enjoyment of learning. At times other than homework, it is great for your child to see you reading or to see you finding out about something, or exploring something new. Learning does not just occur in the classroom and at homework time. Your initiative in going on nature walks, or to zoos, or museums, or open farms will give unspoken messages to your child that learning in whatever form it takes is valued in your family.

Your enthusiasm can also be used to role-model both effective homework routines and enjoyment of learning

Also, while reading and numeracy are taught formally in schools, there are lots of opportunities to use these skills in everyday life. Including your child in the cooking or baking will involve them in using numbers for measuring or examining recipe books to see those numbers written. Going shopping (now that you are more confident to go!) can include them in preparing or reading the list of items as well as reading labels on the products on the shelves. I offer these examples not because I find them easy (I struggle to accept 'help' in cooking and am amazed by the calm patience of my wife, who sometimes has all three of our children beside her at the kitchen counter) but because they are opportunities to make learning fun, and this is the attitude you want to promote to encourage your child to grow and develop into a life-long learner.

KEY POINTS TO REMEMBER

> If you have a choice about childcare, then the best option is usually to mind your own child.

> Other forms of childcare can offer different things to your child, and so choose the kind of care for your child that you think will best meet their needs.

- Your child's minder may have different priorities than you, and so you need to bear this in mind if you have to talk to them.

- Defensiveness is a common response to feeling blamed or accused, so be careful how you approach discussion of your concerns.

- Be ready to accept that your child may be struggling with some aspect of the care, and there is the carer's side to the story too.

- Starting in school or pre-school can be very anxiety-provoking due to the separation from you that is involved.

- You need to take account of your own anxiety about that separation as much as your child's.

- Staying firm, positive and empathetic are the most effective ways of dealing with separation anxiety.

- Have faith that their teacher will comfort them in your absence and make sure to go swiftly when you have handed them over.

- You have to let your child go because, if you don't separate, then they can't move on emotionally.

- Once they have started school, make an afternoon routine that includes a consistent time, place and procedure for doing their homework.

- Role-model an interest in learning by reading and exploring your environment.

- Learning can be incorporated into many household activities as long as you include your children in those tasks.

ACKNOWLEDGEMENTS

I had often thought about writing a book. The concept was classified, in my thinking and career aspirations, under 'Grand Plans to Consider'. It was shelved, peacefully, gathering dust alongside one of my other grand plans: learning to surf. Then, somewhat suddenly, over a summer, I managed to write this book and learn to surf. In both instances I have other people to thank for the inspiration to stop thinking and take action.

For the book bit I want to thank Michael and Patricia at Penguin Ireland for launching me into the world of authorship and for guiding me along the way.

I have my family to thank for getting me up to surf.

I hadn't realized how much work was involved in writing a book. Naivety, in these circumstances, is a protective thing. In retrospect, I'm glad that I have just gone and done it without really planning it. If I had known the process involved before I began I might have been a little too daunted to start. I want to thank Breda, Emma and Patrick for their practical help and support in the achievement of the book.

As they looked at the computer screen over my shoulder while I typed my children made helpful and insightful comments such as 'It doesn't look like a book, Dad, it's just a load of words.' At least it looks like a book now. So, thanks, Conall, Megan and Éanna – you may not have been able to foresee the finished product, but it didn't stop you having faith in me and putting up with not seeing as much of me as normal.

There is a cruel irony in the fact that writing a book about how to make the most of being a parent involved being so absent from my usual role as Dad. Michèle, my wife, recognized this from early on but didn't begrudge it (at least not too often). This is the moment that I would love to be able to create illustrative words and erudite prose to describe properly how the generosity of her spirit and love contributed, so significantly, to the creation of this book. In some ways it is a pity that my prose fails me because I think she richly deserves something beautiful to be said. In other ways, it is no bad thing, because I know she'll understand when I say, Michèle, thanks for everything.